English ⊞ Heritage
Book of
Danebury

Barry Cunliffe

B. T. Batsford Ltd/English Heritage
London

the
UNIVERSITY
of
GREENWICH

Typeset by
Goodfellow & Egan Phototypesetting Ltd,
Cambridge
and printed in Great Britain by
The Bath Press, Bath

Published by B. T. Batsford Ltd
4 Fitzhardinge Street, London W1H 0AH

A CIP catalogue record for this book is available
from the British Library

ISBN 0 7134 6885 8 (cased)
ISBN 0 7134 6886 6 (limp)

Contents

Illustrations

Colour plates

Preface

The first version of this book was published in 1983 under the title *Danebury: Anatomy of an Iron Age Hillfort*. At that time the excavation, which had begun in 1969, was in its fifteenth season and we were just planning the last five-year programme which brought the field-work to completion in the early autumn of 1988. Twenty annual seasons of four to six weeks employing 40–50 people a day inevitably produced a mass of data, some repetitive but much of it new and unexpected. Such an input of research effort has meant that Danebury is now the most thoroughly studied hillfort in Britain and features large in current discussions about the British Iron Age. But as the work progressed it became clear that to appreciate the emerging story of Danebury we needed to know far more about the cultural landscape in which it was set. Accordingly, immediately the Danebury programme ended we began a new Danebury Environs Programme, funded by English Heritage and Hampshire County Council, to study a range of sites within the region, in order to try to understand the development of ancient societies living on the Hampshire chalkland from 800 BC–AD 100. The Danebury Environs Programme began in 1989 and is scheduled to last for seven field seasons. At the moment of writing therefore we are preparing for the fourth season's work.

The present book is essentially an updated version of the earlier volume. It has been extensively revised and new material added, but to keep it within the structure and length of the series to which it now belongs some sections have had to be omitted most notably those dealing with techniques of excavation, recording and dating. While we can still fairly call it the *Anatomy of an Iron Age Hillfort* the tools of the surgeon are now less in evidence.

It goes without saying that a project of this size is a team effort. Besides the hundreds of people who have taken part in the physical excavation about 40 specialists have helped prepare the material for publication, and all the time, discreetly in the background, there has been the guiding hand of the Danebury Trust whose enthusiasm and strength of purpose have ensured the project's success.

The present volume relies heavily on illustrative material published in the four excavation reports (p. 122). Most of the line work was prepared by Mike Rouillard, Alison Wilkins and Simon Pressey. **39**, **43** and **48** were drawn by Christina Unwin and **50** and **colour plates 3, 6** and **9** by Karen Guffog. The photographs are from the archives of the Danebury Trust and the Institute of Archaeology, Oxford.

Barry Cunliffe
Oxford
13.vi.92

1

Hillforts: progress towards an understanding

On a wet afternoon late in November 1859 Sir Augustus W. Franks, Director of the Society of Antiquaries of London, stood in the tree-covered centre of Danebury Ring, overlooking the famous Stockbridge racecourse, while workmen shovelled out the contents of an Iron Age pit. He had been called in by the local vicar, the Revd Walter Blunt, after the pit had been found by labourers digging for rabbits, and the two men looked on in keen anticipation as work proceeded. A few years before some iron objects, a bone comb and a silver coin had been found, but the spoils of this particular afternoon's activity proved to be meagre – bones of cattle and goat and a few sherds of coarse dark-coloured pottery. Franks was not disappointed. After all practically nothing was known of these hillforts and the pit itself, 8 feet deep and 4 feet 10 inches in diameter, was a noteworthy discovery even though no one really knew what these features were for. On his return to London, Franks completed his report to the Society with these words, 'The very unfavourable state of the weather prevented any further excavations, but I trust that my visit will lead to a careful survey being made of this interesting spot, and I may be able at some future time to accept Mr Blunt's kind proposal to make researches there on a more extended scale.' This however was not to be and Danebury remained untouched for more than a hundred years.

Early studies of hillforts

Hillforts held a fascination for the early antiquaries. Among the largest of our ancient man-made structures, dominating the sky lines, they were redolent of the power and the conflicts of past ages – but how far back? In the Middle Ages they were assigned to folk heroes like Arthur or the giant Bevis or to Julius Caesar, Alfred or the Danes. But by the eighteenth century, when so many of the county histories were written, it was generally believed that hillforts were the work of the Romans.

If the eighteenth century was the time for observation and speculation, the nineteenth century bred men who felt the need for new evidence to check their fancies and their theories. For them the best way to acquire that evidence was to dig. The most obvious targets for the early excavators were the Bronze Age barrows that cluttered the southern British landscape in such profusion. In Wiltshire, Sir William Colt Hoare dug 379 in the space of ten years in an attempt to advance the study of prehistory but in the end had to admit 'total ignorance as to the authors of these sepulchral memorials; we have evidence of the very high antiquity of our Wiltshire barrows, but none respecting the tribes to whom they appertained, that can rest on solid foundations.' Colt Hoare was one of the first British prehistorians to become aware of how grudgingly the past yields its secrets, and yet the only way forward was by excavation.

Barrows could be picked off easily before Sunday lunch, according to the standards of the times, but hillforts provided a more difficult problem and for this reason they tended to escape the spade for a little longer. One of the first to receive serious attention was Worlbury, jutting out on a promontory into the Bristol Channel just above Weston-super-Mare. It was first described in Collinson's *History of Somerset*, published in 1791, where, as one might expect, it was called 'Caesar's Camp'. In 1818 a local antiquary, the Revd J. Skinner, dug a few inconclusive holes inside the defences and there matters rested until 1851, when a group of local enthusiasts, led by the Revd Francis Warre, began what can fairly be regarded as the first serious exploration of a British hillfort, excavating an impressive total of 93 pits and finding, for their pains, a miscellaneous collection of domestic debris. The details of this work, together with the results of further excavations on the defences, were brought together by C. W. Dymond and published in 1886 in a substantial volume devoted solely to Worlbury.

The early work at Worlbury became widely known among antiquarians and inspired others to explore their local forts. An outstanding campaign was organized by Col. Augustus Henry Lane Fox. (Later, when a Major-General, he changed his name to Pitt Rivers on inheriting an estate on Cranborne Chase where he carried out and published a series of remarkable excavations.) In 1867, however, early in his archaeological career, Lane Fox was concerned with the hillforts of Sussex, and in February of 1868 he read a paper to the Society of Antiquaries entitled 'An examination into the character and probable origin of the Hill Forts of Sussex'. While staying in Brighton in September he had examined many of the forts of the South Downs, as a result of which he felt able to reject the still widely held view that they were Roman and to conclude:

> There does not . . . appear to me to be anything, either in the position of the gateways or of the works themselves, that is incompatible with the hypothesis of their having been isolated works, erected by several distinct tribes as a protection against the incursions of their neighbours. Such a state of society is more in accordance with what we find to be the early conditions of savage life in every part of the world. We know that in the time of Caesar the several tribes of the Gauls and Britons were always at war with each other until they united to repel his attacks; and the lower we descend in the scale of civilization the more invariably we find that races were split into tribes and families, living side by side in conditions of perpetual hostility.

Here, then, is a clear vision, not only of the pre-Roman date of the forts but of how they reflected the social systems of the times. As in so much of his archaeological work, Lane Fox was bringing his incisive military mind and his extensive anthropological knowledge to bear on a problem which previously had been befuddled by clergymen steeped in the Classics.

Not content with merely observing the earthworks and offering informed speculation, Lane Fox decided to test his views by excavation, beginning with trial work at Cissbury and Highdown and turning, in 1877–8, to a more extended programme at Mount Caburn, near Lewes. The range of artefacts found at the Caburn, including Celtic coins, confirmed the view that many, if not most, of the forts, were occupied in the Iron Age, though, with a correct caution, Lane Fox left open the possibility that some may have been first erected in earlier times. Nor was his mind closed to the possibility that some of the forts might have been built later. At Caesar's Camp, Folkestone, where he excavated in the summer of 1878, he found conclusive proof of the medieval date of the earthworks and in his report reminded his audience:

> it is a common practice to connect together in point of time objects which bear a general resemblance to one another, and this is justified by the continuity and conservatism observable in pre-history and non-historic remains generally; but it is the part of the anthropologist to distinguish those points of similitude which being the result of like causes may belong to any period in which like causes may have occurred.

It was becoming clear, then, that hillforts were more complex than they might superficially appear to be: to begin to understand them and their relevance to British prehistory, it would be necessary to excavate more of them. So the great spate of hillfort digging began. In Wiltshire a programme of excavation was instigated by Maud Cunnington. Between 1907 and 1932 she examined Olivers Camp, Knap Hill Camp, Casterley Camp, Lidbury Camp, Figsbury Rings, Chisbury Camp, Chisenbury Trendle and Yarnbury, publishing each with great efficiency in the *Wiltshire Archaeological Magazine*. Meanwhile in Sussex, a Brighton doctor and enthusiastic amateur archaeologist, E. Cecil Curwen, carried on Lane Fox's work excavating the Caburn, The Trundle, Cissbury, Hollingbury and Thundersbarrow between 1926 and 1932. Work in Hampshire started at about the same time with the excavation of St Catherine's Hill and continued throughout the

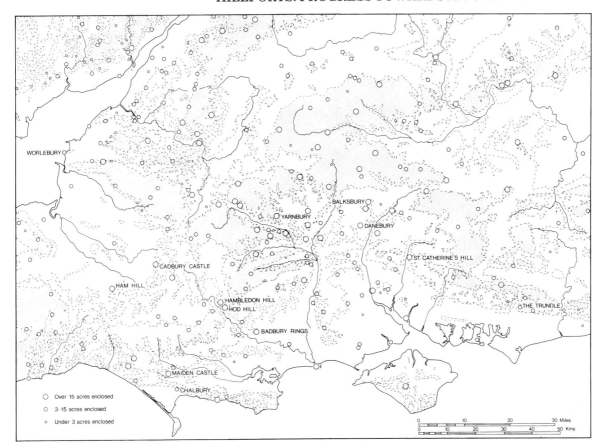

1 *The hillforts of southern Britain. All sites shown are likely to have been in use in the first millennium BC, though not all at the same time. (Information based on the Ordnance Survey Map of Southern Britain in the Iron Age, 1962.)*

1930s at Buckland Rings, Quarley Hill, Bury Hill and Balksbury under the energetic guidance of Christopher Hawkes. To continue with county lists of this kind would be tedious but the three quoted are sufficient to show something of the hillfort mania that gripped British archaeology in the 1920s and 1930s. By 1940 about 80 forts had been dug into (**1**).

The first serious attempt to bring together all the available evidence in a nation-wide synthesis was presented in a paper published by Christopher Hawkes in the journal *Antiquity* in 1931 and called simply 'Hill forts'. It was written at a time when prehistorians believed that the British Isles had been subjected to a series of massive folk movements from continental Europe each of which caused major cultural dislocations. Invasionist hypotheses of this kind

are no longer widely accepted as adequate explanation for cultural change, but at the time these ideas provided a plausible model against which to interpret archaeological evidence. After all, the view that there had been large-scale invasions in the prehistoric period was a logical back-projection of the historical period with its invasions of Normans, Vikings, Saxons and Romans; and Caesar, writing of Britain in the first century BC, talked of incursions of Belgae from northern France and the Low Countries into the south-east of the country. It was against this background that Christopher Hawkes wrote. He envisaged a movement of Celts from central and northern Europe spreading into the south-east of Britain in the sixth century BC and fusing with the locals to form the Iron Age A culture. At this stage a rash of hillforts appeared.

It seems that while war was a danger which had to be reckoned with and demanded fortifications, its outbreak was in fact exceptional. In the more normal times of peace,

9

permanently inhabited forts could be allowed to fall out of repair, and some 'camps of refuge' were altogether deserted . . . But the permanent presence of so many great ramparts was justified, for as there were no doubt constant tribal bickerings, warfare must always have been liable to spring from the background into the foreground of existence.

The next wave of invaders arrived early in the fourth century. Coming from Spain and Brittany they thrust into the western parts of Britain, spreading into Dorset and the Cotswolds, where they built massive multivallate hillforts. A little later, in the third century, immigrants from Gaul entered the north-east of Britain, from Yorkshire to Cambridgeshire. These two groups Hawkes called Iron Age B.

Finally, some time about 75 BC the Belgic invaders entered the Thames Valley and Kent, spreading into Essex, while a little later, as a result of Caesar's thrust through Gaul, refugees from northern France landed on the shores of the Solent moving into central southern Britain: these were the Iron Age C peoples. This was seen as a period in which political power was concentrated in the hands of fewer and fewer chieftains and in consequence hillforts, which represented a simpler, tribal system, declined and disappeared. In their place large fortified towns like Verulamium and Camulodunum appeared, usually in low-lying situations commanding river crossings. In territory which fringed the areas of Iron Age C penetration, such as Dorset, the continuation of old-style hillforts marked native resistance to the Belgic penetrations.

This, in broad outline, was the scheme which Christopher Hawkes put forward in 1931 to explain the hillfort phenomenon. It was simple, elegant and neatly contained, within a single hypothesis, all the data then available. With minor alterations it was to serve archaeology well for thirty years.

The hillfort was seen as a symbol of tribalism and a place of refuge in times of stress and in consequence virtually all the excavation effort during the 1920s and 1930s was focused on defences: sections were cut through ramparts and ditches, and entrances were stripped of their turf and overburden. The reasoning was simple enough: since the prime function of a hillfort was believed to be defence, the struc-

tural development of the defences would reflect the history of the fort. Another reason for this approach lay in the organization of archaeology in the 1920s and 1930s. For the most part it was a largely amateur pursuit. There were a few professionals, like Hawkes, who was on the staff of the British Museum, but pioneers like Cecil Curwen and Maud Cunnington were part-timers, though their excavations and publications were of the very highest standard. In short, there was no infrastructure to maintain a more expansive programme. Work was led by inspired individuals using what limited financial resources they could raise from their friends or their local societies. A hillfort would be chosen for attention, a group of enthusiasts, perhaps strengthened by a few labourers, amassed, and for a week or two in the summer trenches were cut through the defences. When the fieldwork was over and the trenches were refilled, the report would be written in the winter and a new site chosen as the scene for the next summer's activities. It was unusual for a site to be tackled over several years.

This method of approach had many advantages: it provided a useful sample of evidence from a large number of sites; rapid publication meant that new information was quickly disseminated; and the work, because of its scale, was not particularly destructive of the potential evidence protected by the soil. It was precisely what was needed at the time. The main disadvantage, in pure research terms, was that by asking the same limited range of questions about defences, the same type of answers were produced and research on the broader front tended to stagnate.

Mortimer Wheeler and Maiden Castle

A major breakthrough came in 1934 when Mortimer Wheeler decided to excavate the vast and dramatic hillfort of Maiden Castle in Dorset. Wheeler was a professional archaeologist of unsuppressible energy and vision. He saw that if British archaeology was to advance, rather than to continue to collect more of the same kind of data, it had to establish a new professionalism and to design research programmes calling for an input on a greatly increased scale. With this in mind, in the early 1930s he had undertaken large-scale excavations at the Iron Age and Roman city of Verulamium, near St Albans. Techniques of excavation and recording had been improved and a young professional and student staff trained. When the work at Verulamium came to an end Wheeler decided to move his team to Maiden Castle.

One of the main attractions of Maiden Castle was its great size – it appealed to Wheeler's sense of challenge. Moreover the excavation of such a prestigious site would not go unnoticed. But there were also sound academic reasons. As Wheeler explained:

> South of the Thames and between the Hampshire Avon and the Exe – an area about 90 miles by 40 miles – the Ordnance map shows over seventy of these sites still visible on the surface, and others are known to have been destroyed. Of these sites, a number, notably in Wiltshire, had been 'sampled' to a greater or less extent, and substantive work had been carried out in the east at Hengistbury Head and in the west at Hembury Fort; but in the great central area, where Maiden Castle is the outstanding monument, no methodical work on any considerable scale had yet been attempted. A large and important cultural province thus remained unsystematized, and much miscellaneous material found here and there within its borders was devoid of scientific content. The problem was one which found a natural focus in the great Dorset earthwork.

Here, then, was a concise statement of what he was about – his research design.

For four summers Wheeler's team laboured on the fort. The defences were sectioned and the structural development of the site elucidated, the east entrance was thoroughly examined and two substantial areas were excavated inside the defences. Not only was the scale of the excavation a considerable advance on what had gone before, but the careful stripping of areas in the interior was virtually unheard of. In doing this Wheeler showed that the fort had been densely occupied for hundreds of years. In the central area this could be seen in the complex intercutting of storage pits, post-holes and drainage gullies, but against the ramparts, where soil tended to accumulate, he was able to demonstrate the existence of superimposed house floors representing constant rebuildings in the sheltered position protected by the rampart mass. Emboldened by this new evidence Wheeler began to speak of the Iron Age 'hill-towns' of Wessex.

Knowledge of the interiors of hillforts had hitherto been very sparse. Warre had excavated pits in Worlbury and similar pits had been uncovered by Lane Fox, and later by Curwen, in Mount Caburn. To these can be added Hengistbury Head, flanking Christchurch harbour, where J. P. Bushe-Fox had carried out an extensive programme of trial trenching in 1911–12 and found hearths, ovens and gullies together with quantities of occupation debris. But in spite of all this it was still a widely held belief that hillforts were places of temporary refuge. Wheeler's work at Maiden Castle showed, conclusively, for the first time, that some at least were well-organized settlements, intensively occupied over a long period of time.

The excavation of Maiden Castle was part of a well-orchestrated programme of research. Two neighbouring forts, Poundbury, near Dorchester, and Chalbury, just north of Weymouth, were both sampled. The work at Chalbury was on a reasonable scale (though halted prematurely by the outbreak of war) and involved the excavation of parts of the settlement within the defences where again intensive occupation was found. But Wheeler was now thinking more widely:

> it had become increasingly clear to us that whatever the insular contribution, we could not place the results of our work in a sizeable context without some examination of the material – structural and other – across the Channel.

Preliminary reconnaissance in 1935 and again in 1936–7 in Brittany and Normandy convinced him that many answers to the problems he had raised in Britain could be provided only by a thorough survey and a programme of excavation, undertaken in north-western France:

> In the course of our work at Maiden Castle I had come to the conclusion that the multiplication of lines of defence at that and other sites had resulted, as indeed one might expect, from the introduction of new and foreign modes of attack; and now, in the whole of north-western France it was at once apparent that only in southern Brittany was the same phenomenon emphatic. It became therefore one of our main aims to test this observation by further ground-survey and by selective excavation.

This he did, and in the summers of 1938 and 1939 he and his colleagues surveyed the forts of a vast tract of north-western France from the Loire mouth to the Somme, excavating, on a sample basis, no less than five sites. It was a brilliantly successful project carried out with all the panache and skill for which Wheeler has become justly famous.

By the outbreak of the Second World War hillfort studies had become immensely popular, not least because of the inspiration given by Wheeler's Maiden Castle work. A broad historical framework had been established, public enthusiasm had been fired by the discovery of a dramatic war cemetery in the gate of Maiden Castle where the last defenders, slaughtered in a Roman attack, had been hastily buried, and something of the life of the hillfort communities was beginning to be glimpsed from the analysis of the domestic rubbish found on house floors and in disused storage pits. The stage was set for the next advances to be made, but the war intervened.

In the aftermath Wheeler was quickly back on the scene, excavating first at Lulworth, on the Dorset coast, in 1950 and then, in 1951–2, tackling the immense fortified site of Stanwick in Yorkshire. But both projects were undertaken on a limited scale and their results were interpreted within the confines of the old historical model initiated twenty years before. In many ways Lulworth and Stanwick represent the end of the pre-war research tradition rather than the beginning of the post-war era.

New research directions

New aspirations and new research directions did not begin to gel until the early 1960s. By this time it was becoming clear to prehistorians that the historical or invasionist models used to explain culture change were so grossly oversimple as to be worthless; worse still old preconceptions were inhibiting new thought. Archaeologists were turning their attention to more complex, and far more interesting matters. They were asking by what agricultural regimes did the community supply its nutritional needs, how were raw materials and manufactured goods distributed between social groups, what were the social mechanisms through which one group articulated with another, and could the dynamics at work in society be recognized? In short, archaeologists were now attempting to explain the social, economic and political systems of the past using the detritus of these groups as the raw data,

but deriving their models from the anthropological study of more recent communities. To give one example: in the 1930s the distribution of foreign early Iron Age swords in Britain was interpreted quite simply as direct evidence of an incursion of sword-wielding warrior aristocrats from the continent of Europe. After 1960 few would accept such a simple mono-causal explanation. The question was asked, instead, whether these swords could represent a form of gift exchange between nobles and the evidence for social structure was explored to see if gift exchange was a likely hypothesis – was society so ranked? Is there evidence of reciprocal exchange at this level? Could the run-on effects of such an exchange be discerned? And so on. Some might say that this kind of archaeology was becoming pretentious to the point of absurdity, others would argue that it was ceasing to be naive and that the discipline was showing signs of coming of age.

New attitudes to the past began to change styles of excavation. Sampling, on a regional basis, was still being carried out but emphasis was now beginning to focus on the interiors of hillforts, from which archaeologists could hope to find out about the lives of the people, their economies, their houses and so on. In 1960 Stan Stanford began a programme of excavations in the Welsh Borderland with questions of this kind in mind. The first site to be examined was Croft Ambrey in the Vale of Wigmore in north Herefordshire, where, from 1960 to 1966, he carried out excavations each summer. The three gates were examined, the defences sectioned and a considerable area of the interior of the fort was excavated, sufficient to show that the interior, or more correctly some part of it, was occupied by rows of rectangular buildings constructed on a framework supported by four massive corner posts. These buildings, whatever their function, were laid out in rows and were constantly rebuilt over a considerable period of time. Here, then, was clear evidence both of organized planning and of intensive occupation of a hillfort interior.

While Croft Ambrey was being excavated, in 1963, Stanford carried out rather more limited work at Credenhill – a fort in the Wye Valley not far from Hereford. Exactly the same pattern of rows of four-post structures was found and again they were many times rebuilt. As the work at Croft Ambrey was coming to an end, Stanford turned his attention to another great fort – Midsummer Hill Camp – dominating the southern end of the Malverns. Excavation began in 1965 and lasted until 1970 and once more the same picture emerged – intensive occupation, frequent repairs to the gates and parts of the interior densely packed with four-post buildings. In ten years of careful, thoroughly designed excavations, Stanford and his volunteer team had made a major advance in our knowledge of hillforts. It was now becoming evident that many were the centre of large communities, continually fortifying themselves and arranging their settlements in an organized manner. This strongly suggested that they were under the coercive power of a forceful central authority like that of a chieftain or king. The excavations had also produced large groups of animal bones, pottery and other debris, all of which contributed to an understanding of the domestic economy of the hillfort community and their trading links with their neighbours.

Another major project of the 1960s was the excavation of Cadbury Castle in Somerset. Cadbury was the traditional site of Camelot, the seat of King Arthur – the famous folk hero of the shadowy period after the collapse of Roman government in Britain. A wave of public and academic interest in the sub-Roman period led to the formation of a committee to organize the excavation of Cadbury, and Leslie Alcock was appointed director of a project which was to last five years, from 1966–70. Much of interest was found about the pre-Iron Age occupation of the hill, as well as about Roman and post-Roman use of the old Iron Age enclosure, but it was to the Iron Age that the majority of the occupation evidence belonged. Alcock's excavation consisted of several cuts through the massive ramparts, the examination of one of the entrances and the stripping of a large area within the interior. Once more the picture to emerge was of a strongly defended settlement inhabited throughout much of the Iron Age period.

The work of Stan Stanford in the Welsh Borderland and of Leslie Alcock at Cadbury had been carried out solely in response to carefully formulated programmes of research. The hillforts concerned were not threatened with destruction by modern building work or farming procedures and therefore the excavators could not expect state funding. The entire financial support was raised laboriously by soliciting donations from trusts, societies, commercial concerns and interested individuals.

Meanwhile, a serious crisis was developing in British archaeology, created by a spate of development and by the industrialization of traditional farming methods. Unique archaeological sites were being totally destroyed at an alarming rate by such processes as urban development, motorway construction, quarrying and deep ploughing. Funds were provided by central government for carrying out 'rescue' excavations in advance, but the money available was pitifully inadequate and by the late 1960s archaeologists had come to accept as harsh reality that, in spite of their frantic efforts, a vast but unknown percentage of our cultural heritage would be totally obliterated in our life time. To begin with those who shouted loudest got the biggest slice of the funds available, but as the enormity of the problem came to be realized the distribution of funds became less *ad hoc*. To be of maximum value the available cash had to be reserved for those projects for which a clear case could be made on academic grounds and it had to be spent in large enough blocks to enable work to be carried out on a scale commensurate with the academic problems posed. In other words it was no good digging lots of sites on a small scale when the questions that needed to be answered could be approached only by large-scale work.

The rescue crisis, which is still very much with us, had the salutary effect of focusing the minds of archaeologists on research priorities and on the techniques of research. It is no exaggeration to say that the two decades between 1970 and 1990 have been one of the most creative periods in the history of British archaeology. Although much has been, and still is being, destroyed, the quality of excavation, and of the broader research designs within which excavation is being carried out, has improved out of all recognition.

It is, in many ways, fortunate that hillforts have generally avoided the worst horrors of destruction. They are sufficiently dominant not to have escaped notice and in consequence a fair proportion have been given legal protection under the Ancient Monuments Acts. Scheduled sites of this kind are less attractive to developers because of the legal complications involved in any proposed archaeologically-destructive work. Two major hillforts in southern Britain have, however, become building sites: Winklebury near Basingstoke and Balksbury near Andover. Both were selected for large-scale excavation by the government-run Central Excavation Unit, and both have produced results of very considerable interest. Balksbury was occupied for only a short period in the seventh–sixth century BC, later being used as a convenient enclosure for a small Iron Age farm; while Winklebury shows two major periods of defence and occupation, in the sixth and second centuries, with a gap in between. The significant point is that both sites provide a marked contrast to the intensively occupied forts of Maiden Castle, Cadbury and the Welsh Borderland, reminding us that it is dangerous to generalize from such a small sample.

The choice of Danebury for excavation

As has been seen, the new attitudes and aspirations of archaeologists in the 1960s were soon translated into research-based excavations, planned and executed on a large scale. This applies, of course, to a wide range of sites of all periods. It was a useful step forward in showing us how little was really known. At the beginning of the 1960s the younger generation of professional archaeologists had eagerly grasped the concepts and techniques of 'new archaeology', an approach by which it was hoped to arrive at general laws governing man's development as a social animal by using sophisticated concepts, like systems theory, derived from other disciplines. Ten years later most archaeologists had realized that, while the theoretical approaches still held their excitement, the scraps of evidence they were forced to use, amassed haphazardly over a century or so, were just not good enough. If the work of the 1960s had taught anything it was to show how totally inadequate was the data base.

In the late 1960s I sifted through what evidence there was for the Iron Age communities of Britain and laid it all out for review (subsequently it was published as a book). It was possible to amass details of objects, pottery and partial settlement plans; manufacturing skills, trade and exchange, and changes in defensive architecture could be discussed, but it was extremely difficult to move on to more interesting topics like social structure, population dynamics and political change. A threshold of knowledge had been reached, beyond which were only fairy stories of what might have been. But in the large-scale excavations that

were just beginning, and the designing of broadly-based research strategies for gathering data, lay the hope of being able to cross that threshold. It was against this background that the excavation of Danebury was planned.

Reviewing the situation in 1968 it seemed that a useful contribution could be made to Iron Age studies by the thorough examination of a hillfort and its territory, preferably one chosen from an area in which there had already been a number of sample excavations. The chalkland of Wessex was an obvious area from which to choose. An added attraction was that we had just set up a new department of archaeology at Southampton University and a major prehistoric excavation in Wessex would create a useful focus of research where undergraduates could become involved with a long-term field programme. By a remarkable coincidence, at precisely this time Hampshire County Council, who already owned Danebury and had just acquired a route for public access, were wondering how best to display the fort to the public as part of their pattern of country parks which was developing under the imaginative guidance of Colin Bonsey, the county land agent. Christopher Hawkes who knew of this scheme, introduced us and on a March afternoon in 1968 we all visited Danebury together.

Danebury had a great deal to commend it: it lay in the centre of a comparatively well-explored area of downland close to sites which Hawkes, Cunnington and others had dug in the 1920s and 1930s; it was not far from Southampton University; it was owned and administered by a far-sighted County Council; and, it was also a place of great peace and natural beauty – a not unimportant consideration if one is proposing to devote a substantial part of each year to a site.

The one apparent disadvantage was that the fort was covered with mature beech trees. The trees were, however, infected with beech bark necrosis; some were already dead and many were dying. Since it was the Council's desire to maintain the wooded nature of the hill, and this meant replanting, the case for excavation became even stronger, for new trees would eventually take hold and their roots would destroy even more of the delicate archaeological deposits already suffering from the roots of the existing trees. Danebury was chosen, and the first exploratory stage of excavation was planned to begin in August 1969.

2

The Danebury project takes shape

Danebury dominates the rolling downland of western Hampshire. The hilltop on which it sits is not particularly high – only 143m (465ft) above sea-level – but as the surrounding undulating downland seldom rises above 100m (330ft), Danebury Hill makes its presence felt for miles around (2). From the ramparts the view is spectacular: to the east across the Test Valley, the contemporary fort of Woolbury, 6km (c.4 miles) away, sits in the foreground of a panorama which extends across central Hampshire; to the north the horizon is formed by the high downs dominated by the hillfort of Beacon Hill, 22km (c.14 miles) away, while westwards the view is uninterrupted to the heart of Salisbury Plain. Only to the south is the horizon restricted by the ridge of Braughton Down which masks a sharp change of geology where the downland landscape gives way to the heavily wooded sands and clays of the Hampshire Basin.

The Danebury landscape is inviting. Easy slopes and light soils would have made ploughing, using the simple prehistoric ard, a comparatively straightforward task. There was ample upland pasture with dry springy turf suitable for sheep runs, while the river valleys, particularly the Test with its wide flood plain, were admirably suited to provide well-watered meadows for cattle. The steeper wooded slopes and the larger areas of forest to the south would have offered adequate pannage for herds of swine. Wood, straw, reeds and clay for building could all be collected within a short day's journey from the fort while the nearest supply of fresh spring water was probably only a kilometre or so (half a mile) to the west. In times of peace the life of the Danebury community would have been comfortable and assured but

the very existence of the massive defensive earthworks for the fort serve as a vivid reminder that social stress and warfare were an ever-present threat to disrupt the rural calm.

The hillfort occupies the end of an east–west ridge. The approach along the ridge leads gently up to a natural mound upon which nineteenth-century surveyors set up their trig point. From here to the main east entrance the ground is level but confused by innumerable trackways of Roman or medieval date which have scarred deeply into the chalk. Apart from these, all other earthworks visible belong to the Iron Age.

Three distinct circuits can be seen (3). The *inner earthwork* (shown by excavation to have been the earliest defensive work) encloses a roughly circular area of about 5ha (12 acres). Originally it had two entrances: the east entrance, and a south-west entrance which was blocked up some time during the Iron Age. Between the earthworks of the two entrances on the south side of the fort runs another bank and ditch, called the *middle earthwork* while, enclosing everything, is an *outer earthwork*. The outer earthwork is a comparatively slight affair running more or less around the contour of the hill and then swinging off along the ridge to create a linear boundary which can be traced for several kilometres.

The earthworks are visible for all to see and indeed were noted and sketched by several eighteenth-century antiquarians including William Stukeley. Most of them believed that Dunbury, as it was then called, was a Roman fort (4). The slight change of name to Danebury was probably an act of Victorian romanticism, but by the mid-nineteenth century it

2 *Danebury in its present-day chalkland setting.*

was generally accepted that the earthworks were 'ancient British' as indeed the limited excavation of 1859 had confirmed. In 1910 the Hampshire field archaeologist Dr J. P. Williams-Freeman published the first adequate account of the earthworks in the *Proceedings of the Hampshire Field Club*, an account which was to be reprinted a few years later in his famous book *Field Archaeology as illustrated by Hampshire*, containing accurate plans and descriptions of all the defensive earthworks of the county. Williams-Freeman's work was so good that there was little that could be added, except to say that he misunderstood the blocked south-western entrance, believing that the complex of outworks was deliberately designed by the Iron Age defenders to confuse attackers.

The initial research design

In 1968, then, we were confronted on the one hand by Danebury itself and on the other by the current state of Iron Age research. Our task was to design an excavation and research programme within the framework of the various constraints imposed upon us – the level of the available financial support, the amount of time during the working year which we could afford to dedicate to the site and the physical demands of the hillfort clothed as it was with a fast decaying beech wood. The first two constraints determined that we could excavate for a season of between four and six weeks every year. To begin with, while the beech wood was still largely intact, work was constricted but the rapid demise of the trees as the result of disease and, as the canopy opened up, wind damage, meant that we were soon given a comparatively free hand to choose where to dig.

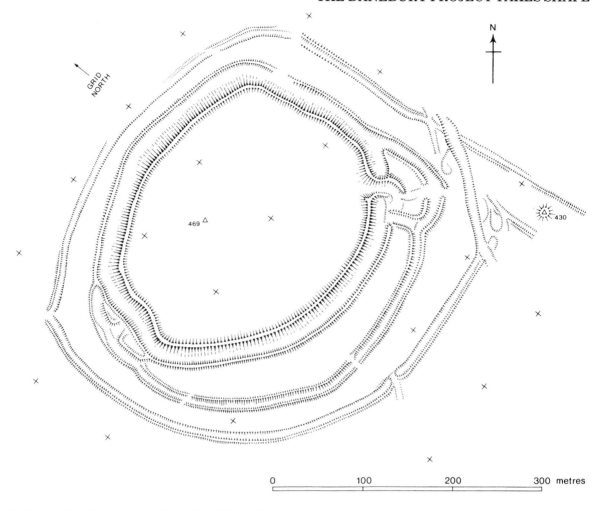

3 *Plan of the Iron Age earthworks of Danebury.*

4 *The Danebury region in 1637 from Camden's* Britannia.

The initial research design was simply to determine site history, to assess the extent and intensity of occupation and to examine the fragile entrance features before the vehicles entering and leaving the site, as an essential part of the woodland management, could do any damage. In practical terms this meant sectioning the defences (1969), excavating the main entrance (1970) and carrying out two area excavations within the defended area, one against the rampart where the stratified layers were thick (1971) and the other in the centre where the soil cover was thin (1972). The results were highly satisfactory: the outline of the site history was soon established showing that the hill had first been defended in the sixth century BC and continued in use to about 100 BC, after which occupation became sporadic. It was also abundantly clear from the area

5 *Excavations in progress in 1973. The deep silts behind the rampart are just beginning to be excavated.*

excavations that the area protected by the defences had been intensively used leaving ample trace in the form of pits and post-holes dug down into the chalk bedrock. Many of the pits were rich with domestic deposits producing pottery, animal bones and artefacts. Another important point demonstrated by the trial work was that while the top of the natural chalk was close to the surface over much of the central part of the enclosure, around the periphery just behind the rampart considerable depths of soil had accumulated and here the more fugitive occupation levels and house floors were very well preserved.

By the end of the 1972 season it was clear that Danebury was an ideal site through which to explore the Iron Age communities living in southern Britain, but only by large-scale excavation carried out over a long period could an adequate sample be obtained to allow us to develop a fuller understanding of how these great hillforts functioned in society. With this in mind we settled down to an annual excavation planned to last for a further six seasons, making ten in all (**5**). The initial target was to

examine a strip across the centre of the site from rampart to rampart and then to excavate a large area close to the main entrance. By September 1978, ten years after the first excavation, the initial aims had been achieved and 23 per cent of the internal area had been examined: it was an appropriate time to reassess the entire project.

The first decision to be made was to publish the results of the first ten years as speedily as possible. Too often large and important excavations remain unpublished for years, greatly hindering academic progress. We fully accepted that it is an overriding responsibility for all excavating archaeologists to make their results available within a few years of the end of their fieldwork programmes. In the event the Danebury excavation reports for 1969 to 1978 were published in 1984, by which time we were deep into the second ten-year programme.

The next stage
The principal aim of the second decade was to acquire a much larger sample of evidence from the site. Two factors influenced our approach. The first was that the rate of tree loss had greatly accelerated and there was considerable local pressure to replant. This required the excavation to speed up since replanting could

6 *The excavations of 1979 with the rampart to the left. All the post-holes and wall slots have been excavated but only a sample of the pits.*

only be allowed in areas cleared by archaeological excavation. The second factor was that while we needed to know more about the internal layout of the fort and the detailed sequence of development, the excavation of pits, of which there were very many, was time consuming and was tending to produce repetitive results. Our response was to adopt a sampling strategy which involved stripping much larger areas and excavating all shallow features, which might be destroyed by tree roots, but selecting only 20 per cent of the pits for excavation using a random number system. In this way from 1979 to 1981 large areas in the south-western part of the fort were examined and tree planting proceeded apace (**6**).

A sampling system of this kind, however, has limitations; not least it prevents the production of detailed phase plans. Nevertheless in the shallow stratified central areas it allowed the internal arrangement of the site, with its system of roads and rows of storage buildings, to be exposed over large areas.

7 *Excavations in progress in the quarry hollow behind the rampart in 1988. The floor of a house is in the process of being recorded.*

DANEBURY   SITE MANAGEMENT

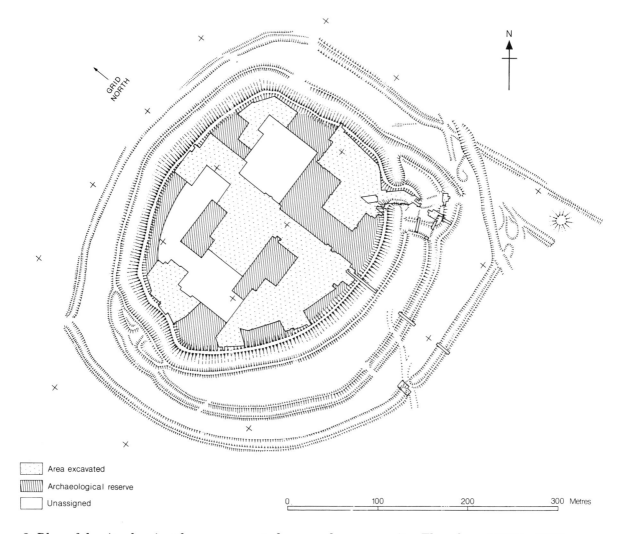

Area excavated

Archaeological reserve

Unassigned

0   100   200   300 Metres

8 *Plan of the site showing the area excavated 1969–88 and the area designated as an archaeological reserve.*

The final phase of the programme began in 1982 when we decided to concentrate on the extremely well-preserved stratified sequences around the periphery of the site immediately behind the ramparts. Here, as the previous work had shown, the structural details of houses with their floor levels and occupation layers, were largely intact and it was possible to work out which structures were in contemporary use. Evidence of this kind is very rare on prehistoric sites in Britain but is crucial when attempting to understand the social structure

of a community. Thus from 1982 to 1988 areas of the stratified peripheral deposits were examined: in 1982–4 on the south-west side where the blocked entrance was also studied; from 1984–7 in the northern corner; and finally in 1988 we returned to the south-east side. In this way large samples of the stratified deposits were examined at intervals around the entire perimeter.

By the end of the 1988 season 57 per cent of the interior had been excavated, 2500 pits had been recorded, 500 storage buildings had been identified among the 10,000 or so post-holes excavated and 70 houses were examined. The sample was large enough – it was time to stop and to leave an area untouched for further

20

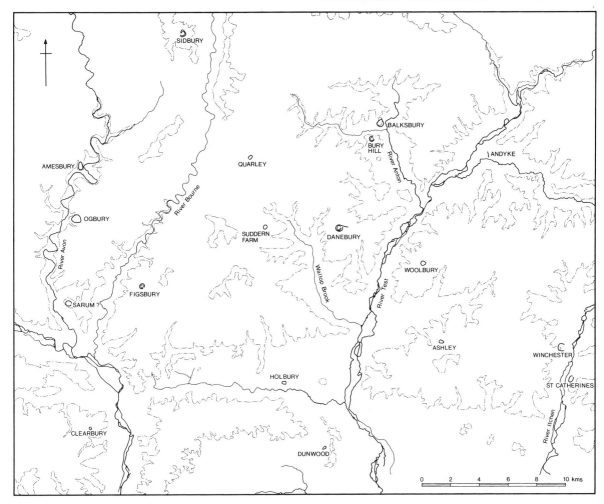

9 *Hillforts and other major Iron Age sites in the Danebury region.*

study (**8**). The second pair of reports, covering the period 1979–88, was published in 1991.

The Danebury Environs Project
The hillfort of Danebury is, of course, only one site in a landscape which had been quite densely populated and extensively exploited by the prehistoric communities of the first millennium BC. An Iron Age farm had been partially excavated on Meon Hill, 4km (2½ miles) southeast of Danebury in 1932 and 1933 and the neighbouring hillforts of Quarley Hill, Figsbury, Bury Hill and Balksbury had all been the scene of small-scale examinations in the 1930s. Moreover, it was clear from the air photographic coverage that field systems, linear

boundaries and settlements existed in large numbers, many of which showed little or no surface trace. To provide an assessment of the cultural background to Danebury the Royal Commission on Historical Monuments produced a detailed plot of all the archaeological features showing on aerial photographs in map form supported by a full typology and gazetteer. The results were of immense value because, for the first time, it was possible to see just how complex the ancient landscape had been and how the different elements, the forts, boundaries, farms, etc, were laid out in relation to each other. In this map lay the clues for understanding the organization of an Iron Age society. It was, however, a palimpsest of hundreds of years of human activity and to begin to decipher it, it would be necessary to sample a number of the key sites. So it was that the Danebury Environs Project was born (**9**).

21

The new programme, which began in 1989, defined a number of key sites crucial to an understanding of the development of the Danebury landscape. A range of questions was formulated about each, and a programme of examination designed to answer these questions. It was decided to spend no more than one year on any site. In other words, the emphasis of the Environs programme was on strict sampling procedures and minimum intervention, structured to complement the extensive (and intensive) programme at Danebury. An added aim of the work was to provide a background of firm data to provide a basis for decisions of preservation and management so that some part of this fast-diminishing heritage resource could be saved before it was too late.

In 1989 the neighbouring hillfort of Woolbury, to the east of the Itchen, was tested to find out something of its chronological range and the intensity of its use in relation to Danebury. Fieldwork showed clearly that the hillfort was related to an extensive system of linear boundaries stretching for many kilometres across the countryside, one branch of which, close to the fort, separated an area of arable from a tract of pasture land.

In the following year, 1990, we turned our attention to the hillfort of Bury Hill which had been sampled before the war. Here two very distinct and separate phases were apparent, the later of which, with its double rampart and ditch in between, contrasted in style to a typical hillfort like Danebury. Here we were concerned to see where Bury Hill fitted chronologically with Danebury because, if they overlapped, it would suggest that they might have been in competition. This proved to be the case.

In 1991 we moved to Suddern Farm, a substantial double-ditched enclosure now totally ploughed out and known only from air photographs. The particular interest of Suddern Farm was that the enclosure was integral with a system of linear ditches and was itself of a type distributed, though sparsely, throughout Wessex, about which virtually nothing was known. We hoped that, in its latest phase, it might be of Late Iron Age date and would therefore follow the abandonment of Danebury, providing a well-stratified sample of material of this elusive period. This again proved to be so.

At the time of writing we have completed three seasons of a seven-season campaign. The enormous amount of new information recovered already means that, at last, we can begin to understand something of the complex relationships of hillforts to their cultural landscapes. The next four years of the programme will, inevitably, augment and change that picture. It is only in this way, through long-term programmes of fieldwork carried out within the framework of a structured research design, that our understanding of Iron Age societies will gradually advance.

3

Man and landscape in Wessex

The geology of the area

Chalkland landscape was extremely attractive to prehistoric man as the density of early occupation in Wessex vividly demonstrates. One reason was that the soil was light and could be broken up with comparative ease using a simple ox-drawn ard; it was also reasonably fertile. In the distant geological past the chalk was covered by thick deposits of sand and clay of Tertiary age. Subsequent land folding elevated a ridge east–west across what later became southern Britain and immediately a drainage pattern became established and erosion began. One set of rivers flowed northwards to the Thames, another southwards to the Solent, cutting into and carrying away the soft sands and clays until the hard chalk was exposed. The result of these processes was to lay bare a vast upland tract of chalk but leaving, to the north in the Thames Valley and to the south in the Hampshire Basin, much of the Tertiary cover still largely intact. In the area later to become the Weald, the rivers bit even deeper, wearing away the domed ridge of chalk and penetrating down into the underlying rocks.

The exposed chalk continued to be eroded by both river action and solution caused by rain water, which is very slightly acid and dissolves away the calcium carbonate of which the chalk is largely composed. Gradually the surface of the land was lowered, leaving an insoluble mineral-rich sediment on the surface to add to the fertility of the soil. In some places patches of clay-with-flints, presumably residues caused by these processes, lie thick on the hilltops.

The glaciations of the Pleistocene period also had their effects on the southern chalkland. Although the ice caps did not reach this far south, the land was permanently frozen and when temperature fluctuations caused thawing to set in, the sodden surfaces of ice-shattered rock tended to flow, creating screes of colluvial deposits to choke the valleys. With the onset of neothermal conditions the land stabilized and soil formation began again. Soon scrub and forest colonized the Downs. By about 5000 BC it is likely that the entire landscape was covered with mixed oak forest, the denser and more luxuriant growth clinging to the clay-capped hills; the more exposed slopes, with thinner soils, being less thickly covered (**10**).

The river valleys varied considerably according to the volume of water they carried. Some rivers, like the Test, flowed in wide flood plains floored with spreads of gravel and alluvium. Others like the Bourne and the Wallop Brook were less substantial but had created well-defined valleys filled with colluvial deposits and gravel terraces. The valley sides and terraces would have been densely wooded while the lower flood plains, when not under water, would have been open grassland.

Much of this general description applies to the Danebury region which, for the sake of this discussion, can be defined as the block of downland between the Test and the Bourne, stretching from the higher downs, north of Andover (over 150m (c.500ft) OD), southwards to the edge of the Hampshire Basin where the heavy Tertiary clays and inhospitable sands created far less attractive environments for prehistoric man to exploit.

Human occupation in the area

Until about 4000 BC the natural vegetation of the area is likely to have been largely undisturbed. But groups of Mesolithic hunters roamed the region in constant search of food and their

DANEBURY ENVIRONMENTAL ZONES

DANEBURY

Zone 1 – flood plain   Zone 4 – woodland
Zone 2 – watered downland   Zone 5 – forest
Zone 3 – dry downland

0   5   10 Kms

10 *Environmental zones in the Danebury region based on soil types.*

presence must have begun to upset the natural balance. The picking of berries and grubbing of edible roots is unlikely to have been particularly disruptive, but camp sites requiring the clearing of vegetation, camp fires which could have got out of control, and the burning of undergrowth to drive animals to the hunters or to improve the browse for wild animals, would have had a cumulative effect in opening up the forest canopy.

By the fourth millennium BC farming communities were moving into the area. The cultivation of cereal crops and the management of herds of cattle and flocks of sheep greatly accelerated the rate of forest clearance. The Danebury region (**11**) can as yet boast no great ceremonial monuments, like the causewayed camps found in the rest of Wessex and in Sussex, nor any henge monuments of the type which dominate the chalklands of Wiltshire to the west of the river Bourne; but 16 long barrows are known, forming two clusters around the locations later to be occupied by the hillforts of Figsbury and Danebury, suggesting

that even at this early date the two hills had taken on a social, political or religious significance – a point which will be returned to below.

One of the raw materials much in use in the Neolithic period was flint. The best quality flint, used for axe manufacture and for making scrapers and arrow heads, was dug out of the chalk in quite sophisticated mining operations which have left their traces in two locations in the region, at Easton Down and at Martins Clump. An antler pick from the Easton Down mine was dated to the early third millennium BC. Together the mines could have provided much of the flint needed in the region.

Evidence of Neolithic settlements is sparse in the area but pits at Winterbourne containing decorated pottery must represent an occupation site, while several areas have produced scatters of Neolithic flints which may indicate settlements.

Neolithic flints were also found on Danebury Hill during the excavations but none has come from a definite Neolithic context – all were found in layers producing later Iron Age materials – but sufficient flint work has been found to suggest that the hilltop was frequented, if not settled at this period. The most diagnostic implements are chipped flint axes and polished stone axes. In addition to these a number of struck flakes have been found, several of which were secondarily worked to turn them into scrapers and piercers of the kind suitable for leather-working.

The status of Danebury Hill in the Neolithic period is impossible to discern from so small a collection. Moreover, the extensive disturbances caused by the Iron Age activity are likely to have destroyed or totally obscured most traces of earlier use. While it would be tempting to believe that the hill was of ceremonial significance in the fourth and third millennia, serving as a focus for the building of long barrows, there is no positive evidence to demonstrate that this was so.

The expansion of crop-growing activities and the growth of flocks and herds led to the gradual opening up of the downland as the forests were progressively destroyed. By the early second millennium there were probably large tracts of open ground used for arable, pasture or a combination of the two.

The extent of open land may well, in part, be reflected by the distribution of round barrows belonging to the first half of the second millen-

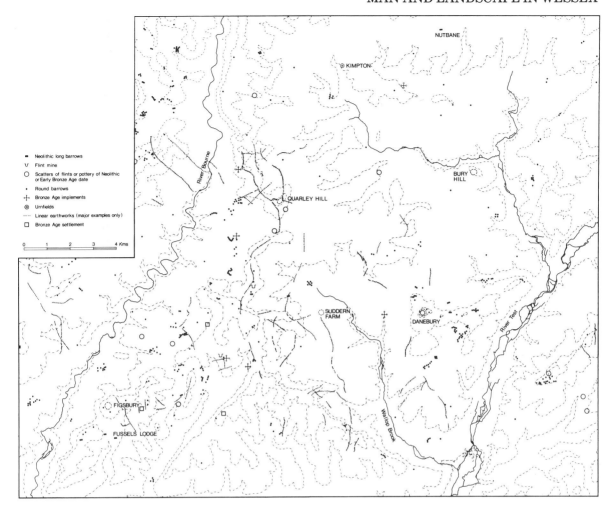

11 *Settlement in the Danebury region in the period c.4000–1000 BC. The map records what survives either as earthworks, or as marks on air photographs, together with chance finds.*

nium (see **11**). Within the Danebury area more than 620 have been listed as the result of a recent comprehensive survey. The fact that 43 per cent of the total are new discoveries noted for the first time on air photographs is a reminder of the destructive effects of later ploughing which may remove all surface traces. How many barrows have been destroyed altogether cannot be estimated. Barrows occur singly, in pairs and in groups of three, but almost half of the total number recorded were found in cemeteries of between four and 15, presumably representing family or kin groups. One of the largest cemeteries lies just south of Danebury.

The reason for the siting of barrow cemeteries must remain largely unknown but there does appear to be a correlation with water: individual barrows and barrow groups run parallel with the rivers Test and Anton and cluster around the sources of the Wallop and Pillhill brooks. One possible explanation for this is that barrow building was concentrated in areas of permanent pasture which would naturally develop within easy reach of water.

Round barrows began to be built in the Beaker period (at the end of the third millennium BC) and continued in use into the middle of the second millennium, some of them becoming the focus for later cremation cemeteries.

Danebury saw some activity during this period. On the hilltop itself there is ample evidence of Beaker period activity. The most dramatic feature was a Beaker burial consisting of a shallow circular pit some 36cm (14in)

25

deep in which was placed a crouched inhumation of a female 20–30 years old. The body lay on her right side, her arms folded towards her face, with fingers close to the mouth, while her legs were flexed with her feet drawn up to her pelvis. Nearby was a beaker, originally, no doubt, containing an offering of food or drink. A detailed study of the skeleton showed that the spines of two of the thoracic vertebrae had been fractured at about the time of death. This kind of injury can be caused by heavy physical labour but is seldom severe enough to be fatal. Another possibility, consistent with the evidence, is that the fracturing was caused by the careless handling of the body immediately after death, possibly at the time of burial.

The burial was not an isolated phenomenon for excavation has produced sherds of Beaker pottery, representing five or six vessels, scattered about the site, mixed with Iron Age pottery. Although it would be possible to see them as the disturbed remnants of other Beaker burials, a simpler explanation is that the sherds, together with some of the quite large collection of flint flakes, represent a limited and short-lived occupation on the hilltop in the period c.1700–1500 BC.

The division of the land

By this time it is likely that agricultural land was beginning to be formalized into a pattern of permanent fields with boundaries marked by fences or hedges. Continual ploughing, causing soil to move down the slope and back up at the edge of the plot, combined with the picking of flints from the fields and the depositing of them around the perimeter, led to the creation of substantial field banks, or lynchets. Field patterns marked in this way still survive in many areas of the Danebury region but it is difficult to say at precisely what date they were laid out. In all probability the process had begun by the middle of the second millennium BC but proceeded in fits and starts for the next 2000 years.

A major phase of land division seems to have taken place at the end of the second millennium or the beginning of the first, when an extensive series of linear boundaries was laid out running for miles across the Downs (see 11). Mostly these boundaries consist of a V-shaped ditch with the spoil thrown up on one or both sides, but at the time it is highly likely that the banks became dense hedgerows or at least were

fenced in some way, and as with more recent barriers of this kind, trackways would have developed along them.

The construction of these 'linears', as they are called, involved a very considerable amount of effort and must have required great communal co-operation, not least since they cut through existing field systems and would also have divided traditional pastures. At the very least they represent the exercise of a strong coercive power. The planning, too, speaks of an overall organization since they are clearly laid out from focal points such as the hilltops later occupied by the hillforts at Sidbury, Quarley, Danebury and Woolbury. The implication would seem to be that certain hilltops had a focal significance at the time and that these later became monumentalized with hillforts and other enclosures.

With the formal ordering of the landscape came the establishment of permanent enclosed farmsteads – roughly rectangular ditched enclosures surrounding the post-holes and pits of a homestead of family- or extended family-size. Two have been excavated in the region, at Thorny Down and Boscombe Down East but others of similar form (and probably similar date) are known from the air photography survey. One of these, at Milston Down, not far from Sidbury, can be seen to be earlier than a linear ditch which is slightly deflected so as not to impinge on the enclosure.

At Woolbury it was possible to show that a linear earthwork had been created just below the crest of the hill running for many kilometres across the countryside. Two earthworks sprang from it at right angles almost a kilometre apart and ran downslope following the sides of minor valleys. Between these lateral earthworks a very extensive system of fields

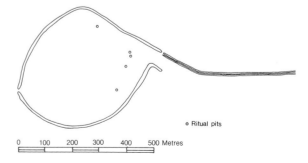

12 *The earliest enclosure on Danebury Hill. First half of the first millennium BC.*

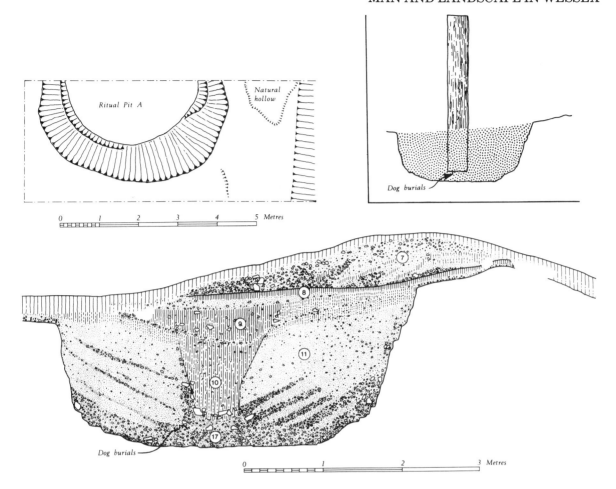

13 *Section through the filling of 'ritual pit' A, with inset of a possible reconstruction.*

had been laid out, while beyond (i.e. south-west of) the southern lateral, the area had been left as pasture and has remained such ever since, allowing the earlier barrows here to survive as earthworks. The exact date of the layout of this remarkable piece of land allotment cannot yet be fixed but it can be shown to pre-date the construction of the hillfort.

The earliest features at Danebury
The situation at Danebury was different. Here the earliest recognizable features are a circular ditched enclosure, known as the *outer earthwork*, and a linear earthwork which runs from it extending for several kilometres eastwards towards the valley of the Itchen (**12**). The enclosure, about 400m (1310ft) across, was defined by a V-shaped ditch, the material from

which had been thrown up in slight banks on either side. The main approach would have been from the east following along the linear earthwork, but there was also a smaller entrance at the west side facing towards the nearest permanent supply of water at what is now the Wallop Brook. It is difficult to know how to interpret the arrangement other than as some kind of stock enclosure for animals. A thorn hedge around the perimeter together with the ditch would have made an adequate barrier for animals, which could easily have been driven up to the linear earthwork and then along it into the enclosure.

It is unclear what structures existed within, but we can be reasonably sure that a series of large pits dug more or less around a contour, inside the outer earthwork but just outside the line taken by the later Iron Age defences, belongs broadly to this period, though it could pre-date the early enclosure earthwork (**13**).

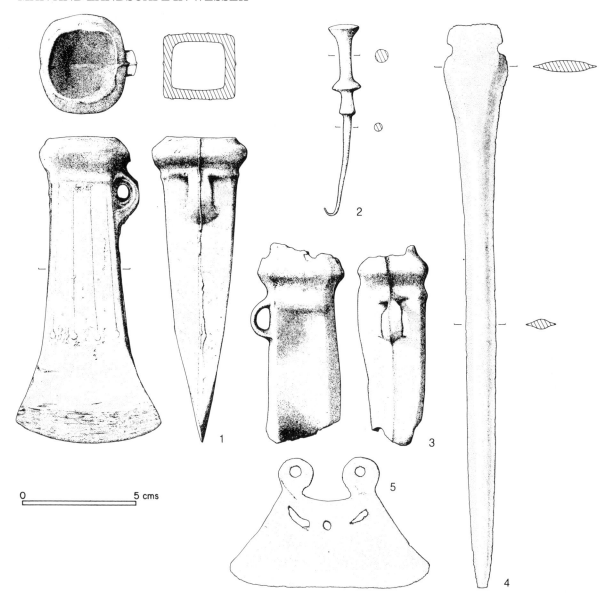

14 *Part of the hoard of scrap bronze buried in c.600 BC: 1 local socketed axe; 2 pin; 3 Breton socketed axe; 4 rapier; 5 razor.*

Five of these pits have now been partly examined; others must be undetected, some of them partly obscured by the Iron Age outer defence. A brief description of one pit will suffice. Pit A was roughly square – 4.4m (14ft) across and almost 2m (6½ft) deep. It had been left open for a while for silt to accumulate and then the bodies of two dogs were placed on the

silt together with an unusual collection of other animal remains including cattle, sheep, pig, red deer, roe deer, vole and either frog or toad. Since, in addition to the dogs, only 20 bones were found, it would seem that a special selection had been made deliberately to include a wide range of beasts. Once in position, chalk blocks were laid over the carcasses and a massive timber, 60cm (24in) in diameter, was erected centrally, silt and chalk being thrown in to pack it in place. Everything about the pit – its shape and size, the animal burials and the post – strongly argues for its representing a series of ritual acts, for which reason we tentatively refer to these features as 'ritual pits'. Another speculation is that the timber, which could easily have stood 3–6m (10–20ft) in height, may have been carved and painted in the manner of a totem pole. Attractive though the idea may be, it is entirely without proof.

The row of ritual pits, some at least with standing timbers in them, implies that the hilltop was being defined in some way, presumably for social or religious reasons and it could be argued that the standing timbers were in the tradition of the late Neolithic henge monuments. The Danebury pits cannot yet be dated, except to say that they are earlier than the middle earthwork which dates to about 400–200 BC. The relationship of Pit A to the middle earthwork suggests that the pits did not long precede the construction of the earthwork but how long a time intervened is guesswork. At best we can suggest that the ritual pit phase belongs to the period 1000–500 BC. The pits may mark the beginning of organized structural activity of communal proportions on the hill; alternatively they could have been dug soon after the outer earthwork was created.

The only other features which may be of this early phase are a series of small 'four-post structures' – a setting of four posts defining a square – which may have served as granaries or, more likely, fodder racks. Some could be shown to pre-date the earliest phase of the Iron Age rampart.

The last 'event' that probably *just* preceded the construction of the fort took place some time about 600 BC when someone dug a small pit and buried a hoard of scrap bronze. The first indication of its existence came in the winter of 1974 when a visitor to the hill spotted an oval-shaped bronze razor in the roots of a tree that had blown over. Nothing more was done until 1977 when this part of the site was excavated and the pit in which the hoard was buried came to light. The contents were particularly interesting since they comprised a range of items, obsolete and broken, collected together for melting down and reuse (14). There were several very old tools and weapons, two massive socketed axes, two broken Breton axes, imported probably as metal ingots from the Armorican peninsula, fragments of a spear and a sword hilt and two razors. The latest items in the hoard were current in the seventh

century BC but need not have been buried for scrap until the end of the century or even into the sixth century. This brings us very close to the suggested construction date of the fort of *c.*550 BC and we must allow the possibility that the hoard was buried not on an open hilltop but in the shelter of a newly constructed defence.

Breton axes are not very common in British hoards (though they occur in their thousands in Brittany), so their discovery at Danebury, together with a well-dated razor (of Hallstatt C type) and British-made axes, is of some note, but what is of added interest is that another hoard of Breton axes was found, early this century, in the valley bottom immediately to the west of Danebury Hill only 1.5 kilometres (1 mile) away. Nothing is known of its context but one tempting possibility is that it was a votive deposit at a spring. It is not impossible that the Danebury hoard was also an offering to the gods buried at the moment that the hillfort was being planned. There is no need to adhere too rigidly to the old belief that these hoards were scrap buried by itinerant smiths with the intention that they should be dug up again and melted down for reuse. It is equally plausible that they were considered to be a form of wealth suitable for dedication to the gods of the locality to ensure their support for a venture as dramatic as the building of a massive hillfort. We can, of course, only speculate.

Although the evidence for the beginning of Danebury as a communal enterprise is scrappy, the enclosure, with its linear earthwork and possible fodder racks inside, shows that in the period *c.*1000–600 BC the landscape was being reorganized on a large scale for the better ordering of the productive systems of the area. The extent of the Wessex 'linears' leaves little doubt that the reorganization was widespread in southern Britain and represents a major reorientation of society towards a more systematic exploitation of the land. Why this should be is by no means clear unless the causative influence was population pressure. If population continued to increase it would explain why, in the sixth century BC, a number of the local polities found it necessary to surround their centres with more massive earthworks of defensive character. At any event, from the middle of the first millennium the landscape began to take on a more aggressive appearance.

4

The fort builders: the sequence established

The first defended settlement on Danebury was created in the middle of the sixth century BC and came to an end, possibly a violent end, some time about 100 BC. Four and a half centuries of occupation necessarily saw significant changes which have left their mark in the archaeological record. In order to begin to understand these changes and with them the social, economic and political dynamics of the community, it is essential to establish a chronology for the site.

Site chronology

The most obvious place to start is with the rampart and ditches, where it might be reasonable to expect to find evidence of periodic redefence. With this in mind, in 1969, a section was cut through the main (inner) earthwork, the middle earthwork and the outer earthwork to clarify the outlines of the main sequence. Subsequent work on the rampart modified and amplified our understanding. The inner earthwork showed a number of constructional phases (15–18). The first rampart, built on the original ground surface, was fronted by an earth-filled box-structure of timber. At this stage there would have been a narrow berm between the front timber wall and the defensive ditch from which much of the material for the rampart had been derived. The timbers would probably have begun to rot within 20–30 years and since there is no evidence of their having been replaced it must be assumed that the later refurbishing of the rampart involved the cutting back of the rampart face to a steep slope continuous with a re-cut V-shaped ditch.

The primary rampart, and its ditch, is designated rampart period 1. It was built in two stages, almost entirely of freshly quarried chalk

rubble dug from the ditch, but was backed in places with tips of clayey soil, possibly the soil removed from along the ditch line and stockpiled inside the fort until the rampart core was complete. The back slope of the rampart had begun to compact and to weather when another

15 *Section through the main ditch and rampart 1969. The further figure kneels on the original ground surface between the holes in which the original revetting posts once stood.*

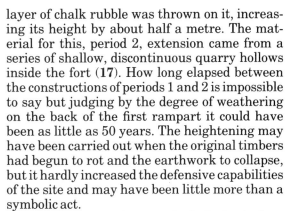

layer of chalk rubble was thrown on it, increasing its height by about half a metre. The material for this, period 2, extension came from a series of shallow, discontinuous quarry hollows inside the fort (**17**). How long elapsed between the constructions of periods 1 and 2 is impossible to say but judging by the degree of weathering on the back of the first rampart it could have been as little as 50 years. The heightening may have been carried out when the original timbers had begun to rot and the earthwork to collapse, but it hardly increased the defensive capabilities of the site and may have been little more than a symbolic act.

After some time, during which the back slope of rampart 2 weathered and a layer of turf formed on it, the rampart was again heightened. The southern defences, between the east and south-west gates, were not substantially altered, the addition amounting to only about 50cm (18in) of silt and chalk scraped up from inside the fort, but on the north and east sides

16 (Above) *Section through the main rampart (1969). The figure crouches on the original ground surface. In the foreground is the quarry from which material for the rampart was gathered. The stages in rampart building can be clearly seen.*

17 (Below) *The rampart exposed in 1988 showing two phases of construction.* Left: *with the third phase removed showing the chalk coating added in period 2.* Right: *excavated to the slope of the period 1 rampart with sections of the tail removed.*

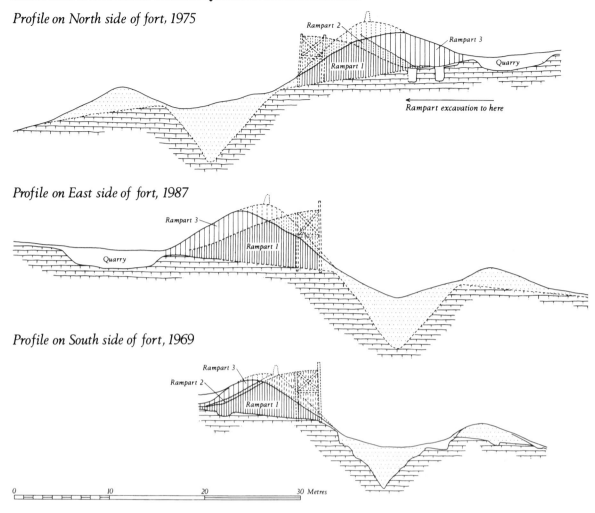

Profile on North side of fort, 1975

Rampart 2

Rampart 3

Rampart 1

Quarry

Rampart excavation to here

Profile on East side of fort, 1987

Rampart 3

Rampart 1

Quarry

Profile on South side of fort, 1969

Rampart 3

Rampart 2

Rampart 1

0   10   20   30 Metres

18 *Sections through the rampart showing the differing profiles around the fort.*

the rampart was greatly increased in volume, the material being derived from a deep and almost continuous quarry 10m (30ft) wide dug around the fort behind the tail of the refurbished rampart. The reason why this sector of the rampart was so dramatically rebuilt may lie in the fact that in the early period (periods 1 and 2) the bank had been much slighter in this sector because the slope of the hill was steeper, thus affording better protection. In period 3 a desire to make the defences of equal strength around the entire circuit would have meant that much more material had to be dumped along the northern length to bulk up the rampart here to the volume of the rest.

It was probably as part of this period 3

reorganization that the ditch was redug to a deep V-shaped profile, 11–12m (40ft) wide and 6m (20ft) deep, with its inner slope continuous with the sloping face of the rampart. The distance up the slope, from the bottom of the ditch to the top of the rampart, would have been about 16m (52ft). It is not absolutely clear how the top of the rampart was treated, but judging by the number of large flint nodules found in the ditch fill and in the silts behind the rampart, the probability is that a breastwork of dry-built flint walling ran around the crest to give protection to defenders.

Defences of this kind, with no wooden structure to rot, were comparatively easy to maintain, but the ditch would have silted as the result of natural weathering and had to be cleared out frequently, the spoil being dumped along the outer lip. Continuous clearing over a

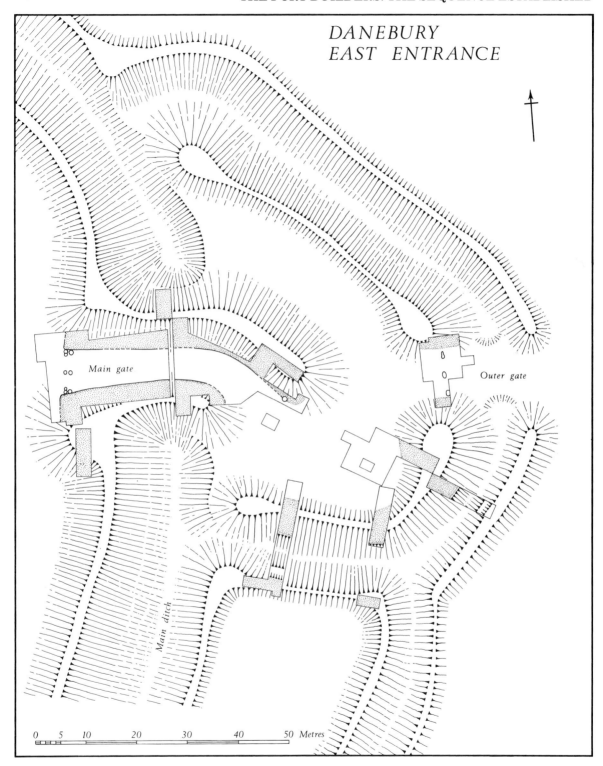

DANEBURY
EAST ENTRANCE

Main gate

Outer gate

Main ditch

0   5   10   20   30   40   50 Metres

19 *The earthworks of the east gate showing the*
positions of the excavation trenches.

20 *The east gate during excavation in 1970 looking into the fort. Part of the flint walling of the last entrance passage remains in position. The road still retains some of the cobbles of its last phase of metalling. The post-holes of successive gates can be seen on either side of the road in the vicinity of the figure and beyond.*

period of time led to the creation of a considerable bank of spoil nearly 2m (6½ft) high and 7m (23ft) wide which, when sectioned, showed distinct tip lines separated by erosion surfaces, each representing a single clearing operation followed by a period of inactivity. In the past, banks of this kind have been called 'counter-scarps' implying deliberate construction for military purposes but this is clearly not the case and the term is therefore inaccurate.

The gates and their chronology
Danebury was originally provided with two gates – an east gate and a south-west gate – but some time during the life of the fort the latter was completely blocked. Both gates were examined to allow the history of the defences to be studied in finer detail.

The excavation of the east gate in 1970 enabled a number of sub-phases to be established. Even now after two thousand years of weathering and erosion the main entrance is an imposing structure (**19–20**). The approach from outside the fort leads first to an outer gate, sited in forward-projecting outer horn-works. These earthworks enclose an entrance forecourt which protects the inner gate set in a gap in the main rampart and reached by an approach road flanked by a pair of inner horn-works of unequal size. What is visible today, of course, is the entrance in its most elaborate and developed form.

The excavation of the gates and the sectioning of the hornworks allowed seven main periods to be defined, several of which could be further divided into sub-phases (**21** and **Table 1**). In this scheme it was not until period 5 that the hornworks, now so dominant, were built.

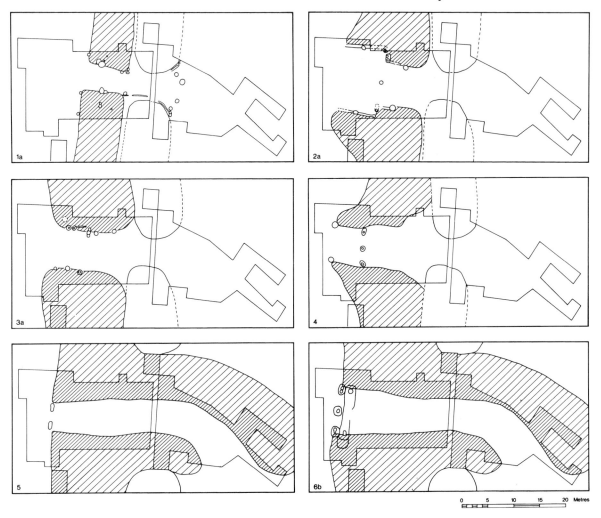

21 *Simplified plans of the successive east gates.*

The earliest entrance (gate period 1) was a simple single carriageway gate, 4m (13ft) wide between the main gate posts, and set half way along the entrance passageway. The rampart ends were revetted with fences brought forward to flank the ditch terminals, each ending in a cluster of post-holes representing some kind of foregate structure. This arrangement would have had the advantage of preventing the animals, driven into the fort, from jostling each other into the ditches. The gate itself, whatever its exact form, was supported by two massive vertical timbers which must have been kept rigid and held apart by a cross beam, possibly supporting a gallery to enable defenders to cross from one rampart end to another. There is nothing to suggest that the gate was hinged nor is there any evidence of a portcullis type of arrangement but one or other of these methods could have been in operation. A simpler explanation, however, is that the actual gate was detachable and was lifted into position and secured by draw bars when the need for defence arose, in the interim being stored somewhere just inside the entrance.

Throughout gate period 1, timbers were replaced from time to time and a minimum of three phases can be distinguished. Gate period 1 and rampart period 1 are contemporary.

The second gate was constructed while the first rampart was still unmodified. At this stage the entrance was completely remodelled to become a broad dual-carriageway, 9m (30ft) wide closed by double gates. Inside the gate line the entrance passage was extended back into the fort and lined with some kind of fencing to form an inner courtyard. After limited refurbishing the gate seems to have been burnt down (period 2c) and for a while the entrance passage was left without gates even though traffic continued to wear the roadway into a hollow (period 2d).

The third gate period is rather difficult to untangle but the wide passage was maintained and there is evidence of the replacement of timbers. This phase is best correlated with the first addition to the rampart (rampart 2).

The fourth period represents a complete remodelling, with the new double gate set well back in the entrance passage which was lengthened at the time. Two inner posts define the corners of the inner entrance courtyard. These, together with the gate posts themselves, may have supported a tower or raised platform above the gate to provide better protection as well as to create a dominating impression on the visitor. The new, imposing gatehouse, set back at the end of an entrance passage, would be very much in keeping with the scale of the outer defensive works carried out at this time.

The fifth gate period saw the instigation of an even grander scheme and is best correlated with the large-scale refurbishment of the rampart (rampart 3). The length of the entrance passage was dramatically increased by filling in the ends of the ditches and building forward projecting earthworks out over them for a considerable distance to create a curved approach 50m (160ft) in length flanked throughout by near vertical dry walling of flint blocks. At the head of the passage was a single gate 3m (10ft) wide. The construction of the inner hornworks created a defensive weakness in that they could be easily outflanked. To obviate this, work began on a pair of outer hornworks projecting forward from the fort ditch, to contain the entire inner gate and the space around it in claw-like pincers. The project was, however, abandoned in a partially completed state and the half-constructed outer hornwork banks were exposed for some time to the weather.

Gate period 6 saw the completion of the project more or less as planned but with the inner gate redesigned to become a dual-carriageway with a gallery or tower above. There seems to have been a change of plan before the gate was finally completed. It remained in use for some while before it was burnt to the ground (period 6c). But the fire did not mark the total end of occupation, for traffic continued to flow into the fort and the road surface eroded into an even deeper hollow which scored through the now-defunct gate post-holes of the period 6 gate. At one stage, in order to arrest wear, the road surface was metalled with pebbles. This last phase is called gate period 7. This brief summary is intended to give some idea of the complexity of the east entrance. How it functioned defensively is a matter for more detailed consideration in the next chapter.

The blocked south-western entrance was only partially examined, but just sufficiently to enable the sequence to be established. Here it was possible to show that the initial gate, contemporary with the first rampart, was comparatively simple but it seems to have been rebuilt as a dual-carriageway contemporary with rampart period 2. The particular interest of this gate is that it was provided at this stage with outer hornworks flanking the approach road (22). Such elaboration is rare elsewhere in Britain at that time. The entrance seems to have declined in use until it was finally blocked when the rampart was refurbished in rampart period 3. At this time the entrance gap was filled with tons of rubble and soil and the causeway between the ditch ends was cut completely away (23). Only the hornworks beyond remained as a reminder of the former elaboration of the early entrance.

The main phases at Danebury

Standing back from the detail it is possible to offer a simple summary of the main defensive and occupation sequence based on the east gate stratigraphy which will be used throughout this book, as shown in **Table 1**.

The *middle earthwork* which defines an elongated enclosure between the two entrances on the southern side of the fort, was sectioned in 1969 and found to consist of a simple dump-constructed rampart fronted by a V-shaped ditch. No dating evidence was recovered but at the east entrance it was possible to show how the middle earthwork turned towards the main fort ditch and stopped, leaving space for a track to branch from the entrance round to the enclosure. When the hornworks were begun in period 5 the entrance to the enclosure was blocked. If a similar sequence occurred at the south-west gate, then the enclosure would have been completely isolated. There are however two undated gaps in the earthworks which

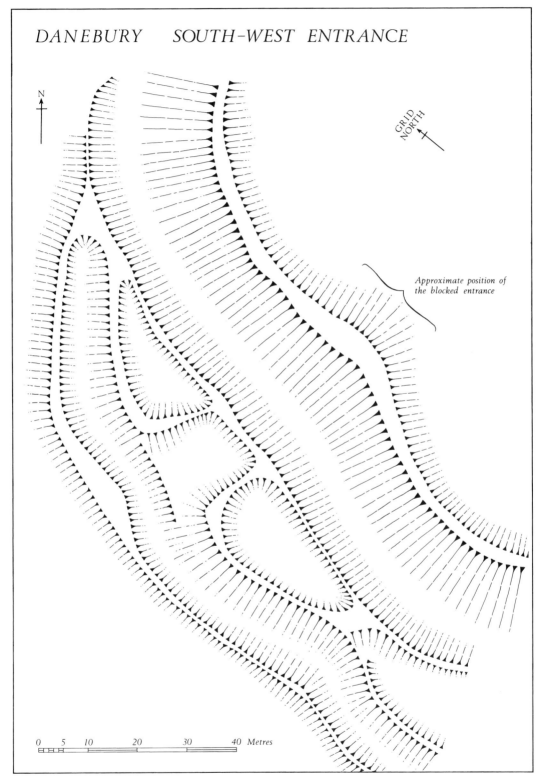

DANEBURY   SOUTH-WEST ENTRANCE

N

GRID NORTH

Approximate position of
the blocked entrance

0   5   10   20   30   40 Metres

22 *The earthworks of the blocked south-west
gate as they are today. Compare with* **29**.

23 *The blocked south-west gate at an early stage in excavation. The figure stands on a soil level which accumulated within the gate after abandonment and before the chalk rubble (behind) was dumped to block the entrance gap. Some cobbling of the early road can be seen. The line of the early road is visible running between the hornworks beyond the fence.*

could have been made at this time to allow cattle and sheep to continue to be driven into the safety of the enclosure. The date of construction of the middle earthwork is undefined but it must pre-date the refurbishment of the rampart in period 3.

Dating the phases

So far, then, we have been able to build up a relative sequence for the defences based partly upon the evidence obtained from the excavation and partly upon observed relationships between the various earthworks. There are two more stages to be accomplished before it becomes possible to consider the development of the Danebury community in relation to contemporary societies: first the defence sequence must be projected into the settlement itself and an attempt made to divide the various elements of the settlement into their different phases, and second, the sequence must be dated.

Assigning the pits, post-holes and gullies of virtually any prehistoric settlement to their

Table 1 The main defensive and occupation sequence at Danebury

Period	Ramparts	South-west gate	East gate
1a–c	Rampart 1	first gate	Gates 1a–c
2a–b	–	first gate	Gates 2a-b
c	–	possible fire	destruction by fire
d	–	erosion	gateless
3a–b	Rampart 2	second gate and hornworks	Gates 3a–b
4a–b	–	diminished use	Gates 4a–b
5	Rampart 3	blocking	Gate 5
6a–b	–	–	Gates 6a–b
c	–	–	destruction by fire
7–8	–	–	gateless

phases is an extremely difficult task unless there is some surviving stratigraphical evidence. Ideally that evidence would consist of superimposed layers. A pit sealed by a layer of road metalling which in turn is cut by the post-holes of a building allows pit, road and building to be put into their correct chronological sequence but without the road metalling, unless the post-holes of the building actually cut into the top of the pit, it would be impossible to say whether pit or posts were the earlier. It is very unusual to find stratified layers on prehistoric sites in Britain and therefore it is usually the physical relationships of features, or the relative date of material contained in them, that have to be relied upon to produce some hazy idea of site development. When features are widely spaced and datable finds are sparse there is comparatively little that can be said.

At Danebury we were particularly fortunate to have exceptionally well-preserved stratigraphical evidence. The most comprehensive sequence was preserved immediately behind the ramparts where conditions were such that layers accumulated quite quickly: a floor level laid in the protected area close to the rampart tail tends not to be worn away by erosion but instead is sealed, and thus preserved, when a violent storm washes down a layer of silt, or when an addition is piled on to the rampart. Even better preservation was found in the quarry hollows around the north and east side of the fort (24). Wherever they have been examined, the quarry hollows have produced evidence of ten or more phases of activity incorporating the structural remains of superimposed houses together with their floor surfaces, hearths, ovens and their contemporary pits. In favoured situations like this it is possible to produce phase plans of the settlement over more than three centuries.

Many clues have to be pieced together to help construct a picture of the sequence. One particularly valuable observation, made in the southern part of the site, illustrates the point well. In this area two parallel road lines were observed, running more or less concentrically with the rampart, both of them flanked by rows of rectangular buildings constructed of settings of four and six posts. Clearly, this represented a major phase in the organization of the settlement plan. Fortunately in one place it was possible to observe that several of the buildings were related to the layers preserved behind the

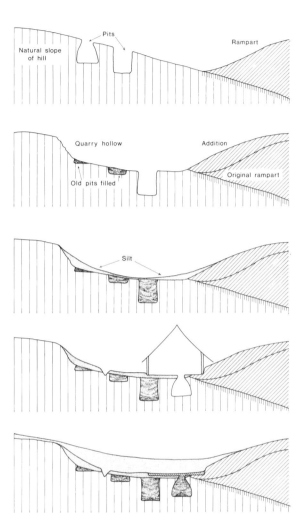

DANEBURY 1973
DIAGRAMMATIC SECTIONS

24 *Diagram to show, in simplified form, the succession of layers behind the rampart. Stage 1 represents the early period (ramparts 1 and 2). In stage 2 the rampart was greatly increased in size with material dug from the quarry hollow and storage pits were dug into the bottom of the quarry. After a period of silting (stage 3) a house was built (stage 4). After occupation had ceased the quarry silted completely.*

rampart in such a way as to show that the buildings were put up soon after rampart 3, and thus belonged to the later occupation. The layout of the roads and construction of the buildings can therefore be seen to be part of the major reorganization of the fort involving the massive reconstruction of the defences.

In the central area of the fort away from the stratified layers behind the rampart large numbers of pits and even larger numbers of post-holes were found cut into the chalk but without any linking stratigraphy. To attempt to fit these into their phases it was necessary to rely on the artefacts found in them, in particular the pottery. Here again Danebury is favoured because pottery is prolific and in Wessex at this time it changes quite rapidly in style and decoration. By establishing the main stages in this development we were able to define a series of nine successive *ceramic phases* (**Table 2**). Pits and other features containing a sufficient quantity of distinctive pottery could therefore be placed within the sequence – at least within certain broad limits.

The main stratigraphical sequence can be directly related to the ceramic phases. Periods 1 and 2 equate with ceramic phases 1–3, period 3 is approximately equal to ceramic phases 4 and 5 while periods 4–6 run parallel to ceramic phases 6 and 7. Ceramic phase 8 represents the last organized use of the site after the main gate had been burnt in period 6c. This correlation is of considerable importance for the simple reason that it enables isolated features to be placed roughly in their chronological context. There is, however, a general limitation: a pit containing a few sherds of ceramic phase 4 pottery cannot belong to an earlier ceramic phase but it could belong to a later one, the pottery being merely residual. This is a real (and insoluble) problem in the case of a feature containing little material, but one producing a lot of pottery can be assigned to a phase with more certainty.

It is possible, then, using various kinds of stratigraphical evidence, together with the pottery sequence, to arrive at a phased development of the settlement and its defences. The next step is to attempt to calibrate each stage in terms of actual years BC. This is particularly important if questions involving the rate of change of the settlement are to be considered. Of the various possible methods available the most appropriate is radiocarbon dating.

More than 70 samples of organic material were taken so that a range of statistical tests could be applied to the dates they provided. After careful assessment it was possible to arrive at the following absolute chronology for Danebury as shown in **Table 2**.

The terms *early, middle, late* and *latest*, set out here, will be used from time to time throughout the following discussion to simplify the narrative. In terms of the overall history of the site they have real meaning. The *early period* saw the creation of the hillfort and its use until the entrances were burned. The *middle period* began with the symbolic refurbishing of the ramparts and reconstruction of the gates, while the *late period* was heralded by the massive reconstruction of the ramparts and the blocking of the south-west gate. It lasted until the main east gate was burnt down. Thereafter, in the *latest period* the use of the old site was sporadic.

Given this simple 'historical' model it is now possible to take a broader perspective and see Danebury in its local and regional context.

The development of hillforts in Wessex

Before Danebury was built hillforts were rare but not unknown in Wessex. In the immediate area the large defended enclosure of Balksbury was already in existence; so too was Winklebury further away to the north-east near Basingstoke. Both sites were substantially defended, though in different ways, and both were occupied by comparatively small communities. Further afield there are other forts of similar date and form: Harting Beacon (Sussex), near Petersfield; Bathampton Down, near Bath; and Bindon Hill near Lulworth (Dorset). All were large (Bindon is massive), all had very considerable areas of open space within and all seem to have been occupied, albeit

Table 2   The dating of the phases at Danebury

	Period	Rampart phase	Ceramic phase	Date
Early	1–2	1	cp 1–3	c.550–450 BC
Middle	3–4	2	cp 4–5 (and into 6)	c.450–350/300 BC
Late	5–6	3	cp 6–7	c.350/300–100 BC
Latest	7–8	–	cp 8	c.100 BC–AD 50

sparsely, in the period roughly 800–600 BC. There were no doubt many more: Walbury (Hampshire), and Ogbury and Martinsell (Wiltshire) share superficial characteristics with the excavated examples but have not themselves been examined. Elsewhere, at Ham Hill (Somerset) and Hod Hill (Dorset), later occupation has partially obscured the earlier features. The list, though very incomplete, is sufficient to indicate that large, early hilltop enclosures were widely, if sparsely, distributed over the Wessex landscape.

Functionally these sites are very difficult to interpret but at the very least their size implies considerable and concerted effort on the part of the community and they are likely to have fulfilled communal functions as places for social gatherings and annual fairs, and as storage and collection centres – all the activities necessary to maintain the cohesion of a large rural community. What is particularly noticeable is that, without exception, all the excavated sites were abandoned by the middle of the first millennium, though a few were reused again for a variety of functions centuries later. If this observation is borne out by further work, then the demise of the early hilltop enclosures must be seen as a major threshold in the socio-economic development of Wessex. The exact meaning of the decline is obscure but it could well represent a change from a loosely integrated and rather dispersed society to a more centralized form of socio-political organization.

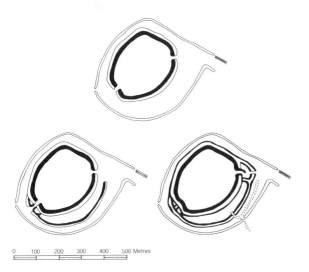

0   100   200   300   400   500 Metres

25 *Simplified plans of Danebury in the early and late periods.*

The next stage is quite dramatic. Some time, probably entirely within the sixth century BC, a rash of quite substantially built hillforts appears all over Wessex. Unlike the early hilltop enclosures these forts were smaller, averaging 5–6ha (13 acres), and rather more strongly defended. This was the stage at which Danebury was built and it was at about this time that the nearby forts of Quarley Hill, Figsbury Hill and probably Bury Hill sprang up, all of about the same size and strength and each able to command equivalent sized territories comprising much the same range of useful resources (see **9**).

The earliest phase of Danebury is comparatively well known as the result of our current excavation. An area of about 5ha (12 acres) was enclosed by a single rampart fronted by a ditch and was provided with two entrances, on opposite sides of the enclosure, between which ran a roadway (**25** and **26**). There were probably subsidiary roads but their lines are not absolutely clear. Much of the central part of the site to the north of the main road was occupied firstly by rows of four-post granaries (or so they are generally thought to be), but these were soon replaced by a densely packed mass of storage pits. Superficially, it could be argued that this signifies a change in storage technique but the argument is weak, for the evidence need imply little more than a minor rearrangement with pits replacing granaries in one area while, perhaps, new granaries were being built in another. Without a total excavation of the site the question will have to remain unresolved.

To the south of the main road there appears to have been a totally different kind of arrangement. Here were a number of circular houses with the spaces between occupied by groups of granaries and pits. Finally, around the periphery of the settlement in the shelter of the rampart, there is some evidence to suggest the clustering of circular houses. The contrast between the north and south parts of the enclosure is particularly interesting. Perhaps what is apparent here is a division between the resident community in the southern zone, each family or family group with its own food stores, and in the northern area facilities for communal storage of surplus grain from the farmsteads outside the fort.

While much can be said about Danebury in the sixth and fifth centuries, comparatively

EARLY PERIOD
550–450BC

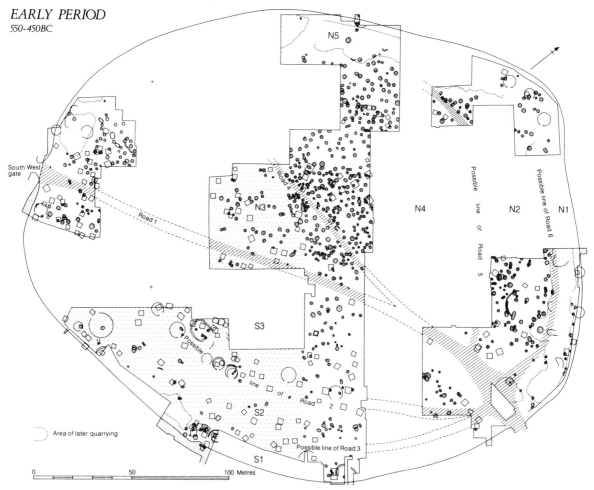

26 *Simplified plan of the Danebury settlement in the early period.*

little is known of other contemporary forts; but in Dorset, at both Maiden Castle and Chalbury, sufficient work was done to show that these early forts were of comparable size and strength to Danebury and were extensively occupied by communities building circular houses and digging storage pits. However, there was little that could be said of the internal arrangements of the settlements.

Returning now to the Danebury region, there is sufficient evidence to show that in the period *c.* 600–400 BC a number of other hillforts, including Figsbury, Quarley, Bury Hill and Woolbury, were also built but it is not certain that they were all occupied in the same way as Danebury nor were they all necessarily in contemporary use. The recent excavations at Bury Hill and Woolbury and the older, more

limited, work at Quarley and Figsbury show that the picture is really quite complicated (and is liable to become more so as work progresses), but on the evidence of the defensive structures it is probable that Danebury was the first fort to be established, soon after 600 BC, to be followed not long after by Bury Hill, where a timber-faced rampart has been identified. There is, however, no evidence here of internal occupation of the kind found at Danebury and the possibility remains that it was very soon abandoned. Some time later, possibly at the beginning of the fifth century, Quarley, Woolbury and possibly Figsbury were defended using a dump-rampart construction without internal timbering. It is not clear whether or not these sites were occupied for any length of time but at Woolbury, where a considerable area was excavated within the defences, only a single pit of this period was found and, as we will see, by the fourth century when Danebury was massively redefended, all three had been abandoned.

To interpret this scant evidence is not easy but it is tempting to see the centuries between 600 and 350 BC as a time of change and possibly conflict when the different polities of the region were attempting to establish, or legitimize, their social positions by building hillforts. There may well have been conflict, and in this context should be noted the burning of the Danebury gates some time in the fifth century. Out of it all Danebury emerged dominant. This is one possible scenario. Another, no less possible, is that the rash of hillforts built in this period served a variety of different functions within a larger polity of which Danebury remained the centre throughout. On balance, the evidence for the burning of the Danebury gates and large quantities of sling stones found behind the southern rampart tends to favour the former interpretation. Could it be that the symbolic refurbishing of the ramparts in period 2 and the construction of the hornworks at the south-western gate at this time were a mark of the eventual victory of the Danebury community over their rivals? We will never know.

The later phases at Danebury

Some time about, or soon after, 350 BC Danebury was refurbished on a grand scale. The rampart was considerably heightened and the fronting ditch redug to a deep V-shaped profile, and the two gates were totally reconstructed (see **28**). This marks the beginning of Danebury's *late period* (i.e. Danebury periods 4–6). The internal arrangements were also reorganized at this time (**27**). The main road continued in existence and two very distinct subsidiary roads were laid out in the southern half of the fort concentric with the rampart. Much of this southern area seems to have been given over to the construction of massive four- and six-post buildings of granary type which were laid out in orderly rows along the edges of the roads. The houses of the late period occupied the lee of the rampart, as they did in the earlier period, those on the north and east sides making good use of the shelter afforded by the quarries. There were also some houses on the shoulder of the hill overlooking the quarries. Groups of storage pits were scattered around the interior; their spacing suggests that they were now in distinct clusters, perhaps relating to individual social groups. The central part of

the site to the north of the main road seems to have been deliberately cleared and the area levelled with tips of chalk spread wherever there was a hollow in the ground left by a partially filled pit. Part of this central area was now occupied by distinctive rectangular buildings which were very probably shrines (see below pp. 71–3).

The late period continued for some 200 to 250 years (350/300–100 BC) during which time there were many alterations and rebuildings, though the broad outlines of the plan, once established, remained largely unchanged, with many of the buildings being reconstructed several times on much the same sites. The implication is of a very distinct continuity under the control of a strong centralizing power.

The defences were not only maintained in good order throughout the late period but the main east gate (now the only gate) was dramatically improved and complex forward projecting hornworks were added to lengthen the approach to the actual gates. The defensive implications of these works will be considered below (pp. 47–8) but another aspect that should be explored is that this display of strength was inspired by social factors such as the need felt by the community to distinguish itself and demonstrate its exalted position to its neighbours. In other words it is possible that massive foreworks at gates were intended to be a widely recognizable symbol of status.

After more than two centuries of intensive occupation, some time about 100 BC, the main east gate was destroyed by fire. After this the entrance was left undefended and the density of occupation within the fort greatly decreased, to such an extent that wholesale abandonment is implied.

Hillforts after 350 BC

The story of the late phase of Danebury, though obscure in points of detail, is well established in outline and can act as a guide to the interpretation of other sites in the region. In the immediate neighbourhood it seems that the forts at Figsbury, Quarley and possibly Bury Hill were abandoned some time before 350 BC, leaving Danebury as the only fortified enclosure on the downland block between the Test and the Bourne. Woolbury, too, seems to have remained largely unoccupied, though a few pits were dug in the interior. A similar picture can be traced elsewhere in southern Britain and is

LATE PERIOD

350/300-100BC

27 *Simplified plan of the Danebury settlement in the late period.*

particularly clear along the downs east of the Itchen where each area of chalkland, isolated by river valleys, seems to have been dominated at this time by a single hillfort: St Catherine's Hill, Old Winchester Hill, Torberry, Trundle, Cissbury, Devils Dyke and Caburn. A similar situation can be traced over much of Wessex. Wherever there has been sufficient excavation it can usually be shown that the hillforts that survived – known as *developed hillforts* – grew out of existing settlements or enclosures. This rise to dominance of selected sites must reflect a significant, and apparently quite rapid, change in the socio-political structure – it looks very much as though there was a sudden coalescence of power in the hands of a smaller number of communities.

At Danebury, as already noted, the new defensive line followed exactly that of the original circuit and this probably happened in the majority of cases, but some forts were greatly extended at this time. A prime example is Maiden Castle where the fort was more than doubled in area when the fortifications were thrust eastwards to embrace the crest of an adjacent hill. At Hambledon Hill, overlooking the Stour Valley, at least two successive enlargements can be traced by a careful study of the existing earthworks, even though the site has not been excavated, while at Yarnbury (Wiltshire), excavation has shown that the original circuit was totally abandoned and a new system of defences built outside it to enclose a much larger area.

Wherever it is possible to check the date of these reorganizations they seem to coincide with a development in pottery styles equivalent to the transition between the middle and late periods at Danebury. They are likely therefore to be of approximately the same date but how sudden was this change it is impossible to say and we must allow that the evolution from densely scattered early hillforts to more widely spaced, developed hillforts may have taken anything up to a century to complete. The archaeological data, at present available, do not allow greater precision.

The century following 350 BC was, then, a period of dramatic change in Wessex when centres of power were crystallizing out, but there is no reason to suppose that they were all of equivalent status, or that the status of each remained static during the next 200–300 years. A more likely model anticipates a complex situation with some forts pre-eminent and commanding the allegiance of lesser forts but with the patterns of allegiance changing as the fortunes of the major centres rose and fell. It is entirely beyond the limits of the present evidence to discern even the broadest direction of such a dynamic situation but the individual forts which have been excavated show a wide variety of patterns. At Winklebury (northern Hampshire), although the early fortifications were rebuilt, the community within appears to have remained small and lacked any sign of careful organization. Danebury, on the other hand, was densely occupied throughout and developed grandiose entrances late in its life, while Maiden Castle grew to colossal proportions with a vastly complex system of multivallate defences and with most unusual double gateways. The three examples are sufficient to demonstrate a range of variation reflecting the very different political positions occupied by these sites in the contemporary settlement hierarchy.

The recent excavations at Bury Hill, only 6km (4 miles) to the north of Danebury have shown that some time towards the end of the late period of Danebury, probably late in the second century BC or early in the first, the old, long-abandoned fort was suddenly brought back into active use when a smaller circuit was defended by a massive ditch flanked inside and out by substantial ramparts. The style of defence differs from that of traditional hillforts and looks forward to the latest Iron Age fortifications characterized by Suddern Farm (p. 118). Inside, occupation was quite intensive and the finds, which include large quantities of horse harness and chariot fittings and an unusually large number of horse bones, strongly suggest an aristocratic warrior settlement. Suddenly then, Danebury, after more than two centuries of dominance, now had to face competition. Who the builders of Bury Hill were and the nature of their relationship with Danebury will never be known, but soon after the long occupation of Danebury came to an end.

The abandonment of Danebury and other hillforts

In about 100 BC the gate of Danebury was burned, groups of bodies were thrown into charnel pits and most of the population departed from the protection of the defences. Whether or not these events were interlinked is a problem for consideration below (pp. 115–18). The aftermath saw Danebury still in use but compared with the intensity of occupation in the previous centuries the scene now would have looked very different. There were no gates, but there was a deeply-worn road, winding between the eroding hornworks to the interior of the enclosure where one of the old shrines probably continued in use. Some sort of community still lived close by but the streets were deserted, the granaries decayed and gone, and where there were once densely packed houses behind the ramparts, silt had obscured everything and bushes were growing. Much of the interior was probably grazed by flocks and herds. By the beginning of the first century AD the settlement, probably nothing more than a single farm, had moved from the centre of the fort to occupy a more sheltered position against the southern rampart where it was to last for a few more decades before dying.

The abandonment of hillforts about 100 BC seems to have been a widespread phenomenon in much of south-eastern England. Why this should have occurred remains obscure but it was a time of rapid social, economic and political change brought about by the sudden resurgence of overseas trade generated as a bow wave in advance of the gradual Roman annexation of Gaul. In the face of such changes the traditional socio-economic system broke down and hillforts became obsolete over large areas of the south. Many saw sporadic use in Roman, sub-Roman, Saxon and medieval times, but by then they had become grass-grown ruins — reminders to succeeding generations of a short-lived but remarkable period in the British past.

═══ 5 ═══
Defence and warfare

'The Celts', wrote the Greek geographer Strabo, 'were war mad, high spirited and quick to battle but otherwise straightforward and not of evil character.' The hillforts of England are, to a large extent, the archaeological manifestation of this statement. This chapter begins with a consideration of the ramparts and gates of Danebury and the weapons of its defenders, and then moves on into the wider Celtic world to explore this readiness to war.

The ramparts
The ramparts, ditches and gates of Danebury, whatever their significance as a means of displaying the prestige of the occupants, were primarily defensive in character. The early fort with its vertical wall of timber, standing some 4m (13ft) in height, backed by a solid earth rampart and fronted by a ditch, would have confronted a would-be attacker with a formidable obstacle. He might have been able to get close enough to set fire to it but this would have done little good because the backing earth and rubble rampart was laced with timbers in such a way that the core would have remained stable long enough for the defenders to concentrate their efforts and avert the threat. The gates, on the other hand, were more susceptible.

In the early period they could have been reached comparatively simply across the causeways (though this might have meant breaking through the outer gate first) and faggots of brushwood piled against them and fired would soon have set the timber structure alight. In fact we are given a precise description of just such a method of attack by Julius Caesar writing of native siege tactics in the middle of the first century BC:

The Gauls and the Belgae use the same method of attack. They surround the whole circuit of the walls with a large number of men and shower it with stones from all sides, so that the defences are denuded of men. Then they form *testudo*, set fire to the gates and undermine the walls.

Although this passage was written 500 years after the first defensive circuit was built around Danebury the technique of attack is unlikely to have changed much in that time. Nor should it be forgotten that there is evidence for at least one of the early gates being destroyed by fire – perhaps in just such an attack.

The reorganization of the defences about 350 BC marks a major advance in defensive architecture. The old idea of the vertical timber wall had clearly proved to be ineffective. Timbers of this size would have rotted through at the base within about 30–40 years and would either have had to be replaced (which would have been extremely difficult) or would simply have been left to disintegrate. The new scheme was a distinct improvement. In essence, a continuous steep slope was created from the bottom of a deep V-shaped ditch to the crest of the rampart which was capped by a breastwork wall of flint. On the south side of Danebury that slope was 16m (53ft) in length – impossible to scale with the defenders standing behind the wall and hurling missiles. Anyone attempting to climb up would be sure to tumble back into the constricted bottom of the ditch where he would be at the mercy of those on the rampart. This type of arrangement – the glacis style of defence – was widely adopted in southern Britain and reached its culmination in the complex multivallation of sites like Maiden Castle.

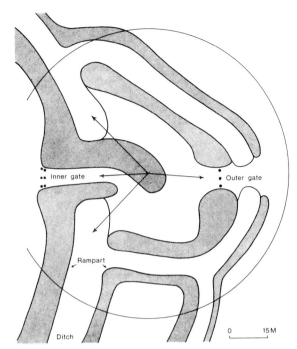

28 *Diagram to show how the defences of the east gate worked. The 'command post' lay in the centre of the complex.*

The entrances

As before, it was the entrances that proved most vulnerable and it is only to be expected that here considerable ingenuity was lavished. The overriding aim was to distance the main gate as much as possible from the foremost position that the defenders could man. One way in which this was often accomplished was to turn the rampart ends into the fort to form a long entrance passage at the end of which the gate was constructed. Another technique was to construct elaborate outworks, but quite often the two were used together. At Danebury outworks were favoured.

The east entrance, in its final form, was a masterpiece of planning (**28**). Instead of being turned into the fort the rampart ends were turned outwards – a scheme which necessitated the infilling of the ditch terminals. The result was to create a curved passageway, flanked by near-vertical flint walling, some 50m (160ft) in length, with the gate set at the inner end. To provide even greater security, two claw-like outer hornworks were built with an outer gate closing the gap between them. The plan was an extremely subtle piece of work, the key to which was the end of the north inner hornwork.

This was more than just a flanking earthwork for the entrance – it formed a flat-topped command post from which all parts of the entrance complex could be overseen, clear sight lines obtained along the main ditch, and the entire approach to the gate kept under scrutiny. More to the point it was an excellent position for a party of slingers to occupy in any attack because no part of the entrance was more than 60m (200ft) away, and this distance is the approximate range within which a competent slinger could expect to pick off a victim with ease.

Enemies attacking the entrance had first to get through the hail of fire from the top of the outer hornworks and then batter their way through the outer gate. Having done this they were in close range of defenders manning the command post. If they survived they would then have to rush along the entrance passage towards the main gate suffering a rain of missiles – from the command post against their backs, from the inner hornworks against their flanks, and from the gate tower in front of them, full face. Attacking the east gate would have been an extremely hazardous operation. That the gate was eventually burnt, presumably by enemy action, is all the more remarkable.

We know less of the earlier south-west gate, because it has not been as extensively excavated, but the outer earthworks are well preserved and give some indication of its complexities (**29**). The gate passage itself was not inturned to any degree but the rampart ends increased in width and height as the gate was approached, and sufficient of the structure was exposed to show that it was set deeply within the mass of the rampart probably with a bridge or even a tower above. In front of the gate a long straight passageway about 50m (160ft) long was created by building two earthworks outwards from the gate and then turning them back towards the fort ditches. The outward facing parts of these horns were fronted by deep V-shaped ditches. We will never know whether the earthworks flanking the passageway ran past the ditch ends to join the gate passage or whether they stopped on the outer lips of the ditch but the latter option seems the more likely if the entrance works were as subtly designed as they appear to be. Attackers approaching the gate would believe themselves to have a comparatively clear run

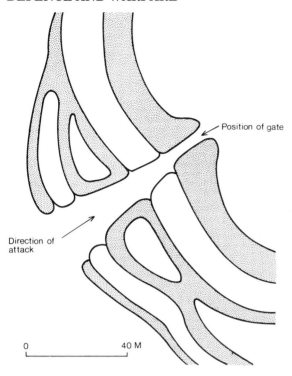

Position of gate

Direction of attack

0   40 M

29 *Diagram to explain the defences of the south-west gate.*

hill, and stored in conveniently sited ammunition dumps, usually close to the ramparts and gates. One pit, near the east gate, produced 11,000, and very considerable quantities were found all along the entrance passage where they had either fallen from dumps on the hornworks or had been hurled by the defenders. In this position they must date to the late period of occupation (*c.* 350–100 BC) but a large quantity of sling stones was also found behind the southern rampart in an early period context (*c.* 550–450 BC) showing that sling warfare was a long established technique. Various methods could be used to dispatch the stones: a swing in a vertical plane, overarm, was best suited to lobbing the missiles high in the air so that they rained down on opponents. A continuous volley of this kind put up by massed slingers would have been devastating to an approaching army, but for closer fighting one or two circuits in a horizontal plane over the head would have been sufficient to send the stone level and fast direct to the target. The problem with this method was the timing of the release of one arm of the sling: it was crucial, otherwise the stone would fly in totally the wrong direction; but with practice a deadly accuracy could be attained.

Although the sling is a highly effective weapon in human conflicts, it is also a very useful item of equipment for people looking after animals, particularly large flocks of sheep. Modern ethnographic parallels throw a great deal of light on this matter. Slings are frequently used to drive off animals preying on the flocks, while carefully placed stones, thrown over the heads of the animals and landing behind them, can be used to drive the flocks in any required direction. There are even communities who use the sling itself to hobble their horses when they wish to leave them untethered. The point of all this is to emphasize that the sling was no doubt a common piece of equipment among farming communities maintaining large flocks and herds and it only began to take on its more aggressive use as warfare became more common – when the occasion arose there was no need to turn ploughshares into swords.

Other offensive weapons in use at this time included iron-headed spears and javelins, and iron swords. Something of the variety of spears available can be seen from (**30**). Each type was suited to a particular function: some were for

to the gate itself, 50m (160ft) in front of them, but what they would not be aware of was that the passageway was not parallel-sided but a funnel, more than 15m (50ft) wide at the beginning but as little as 6m (20ft) wide at the end. A forward assault by massed attackers would disintegrate into chaos as the rapidly constricting passage caused the warriors to bunch, and when they reached the causeway many would be at the mercy of the defenders manning the ramparts. Those who reached the final entrance passage in front of the gate would have been exposed, to the front and on the flanks, to fire from men commanding the rampart terminals and the bridge over the gate. That this kind of gate plan was successful is shown by the fact that the Roman military engineers adopted just such a scheme to protect the gates of their forts.

Weapons

The most widely used missiles at Danebury were sling stones – round water-worn pebbles 2–3cm (1in) across. They were collected in great numbers from pebble beds, which outcrop between 6 and 10km (4 and 6 miles) from the

1 Danebury and its approaches. The linear earthwork running towards the fort can be seen crossing the field in the foreground.

2 The main ditch and rampart of the fort. Though filled by up to 4m (13ft) of silt the ditch is still a formidable obstacle.

3 The main east gate of Danebury in its final state, about 100BC, at the moment of attack (Karen Guffogg).

4 *(Right, above)* Excavation in progress just inside the main east gate. The complex hornworks protecting the entrance can be seen top left with the road snaking around them.

5 *(Right, below)* Excavation in progress on the plank-walled house. The tree root was subsequently removed (with difficulty), exposing the doorway of the house.

6 The houses in the quarry hollow behind the rampart in the second century BC (Karen Guffogg).

7 *(Right, above)* Excavation in progress on one of the more complete skeletons.

8 *(Right, below)* One of the unusual conical pits half sectioned to show the flat flint in the bottom and the main filling of clay in bands of different kinds. These pits were probably used for mixing clay to make daub for constructional purposes.

9 The sanctuaries in the centre of Danebury during a ceremony (Karen Guffogg).

10 *(Right, above)* Terret rings from the harness of Iron Age ponies.

11 *(Right, below)* Complete skeleton tightly flexed placed on the bottom of a pit, close against the side.

12 One of the rare 'charnel pits' containing the remains of a number of partially dismembered bodies. One possible explanation is that they represent the clearing up after a massacre.

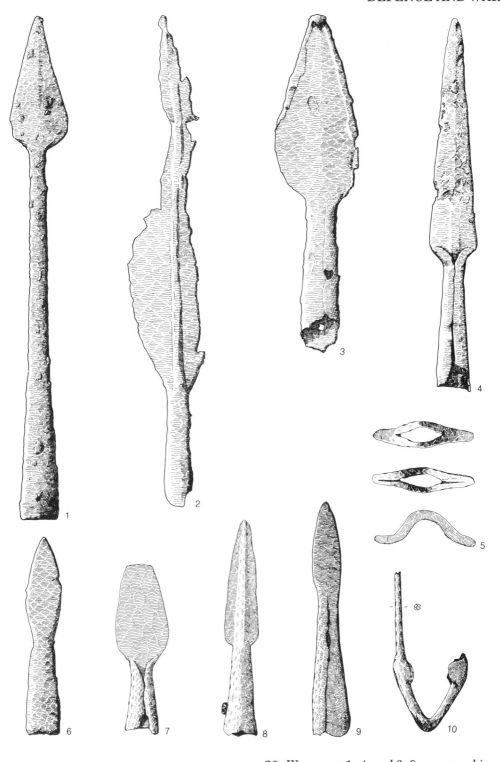

30 *Weapons: 1–4 and 6–9 spear and javelin heads; 5 sword hilt guard; 10 sword scabbard chape.*

0   5   10 cms

throwing in battle, some for thrusting in the attack, others for hunting wild animals. The skill in getting the weight and balance of each weapon absolutely right was no doubt commonplace to the craftsmen supplying them. One specific type, not found at Danebury, is mentioned by the classical writer Diodorus Siculus:

> Some of their javelins are forged with a straight head while some are curved with breaks throughout their entire length so that the blow not only cuts but also tears the flesh and the recovery of the spear rips the wound open.

Judging by references in the Irish folk tales, which reflect late Celtic society in Ireland, the warrior of high status would normally carry one or two javelins for throwing and a heavier spear for thrusting at close quarters. Iron Age burials in northern France are often accompanied by a varied collection of spears and javelins suggesting that this pattern was widespread.

Each warrior of any status would also have carried an iron sword slung in a sheath of leather or wood bound with bronze or iron. Sometimes the bronze bindings were elaborately decorated plates, attached to the hilt and point ends of the sheath. No swords have been found at Danebury but several simple binding strips as well as an iron chape and an iron hilt-guard have been recovered (see **30**). This does not mean that swords were rare but simply that they were too valuable to be lost or discarded.

The Celtic warrior dressed in his finery would have been an awe-inspiring sight. Diodorus Siculus provides a vivid description:

> Their armour includes man-sized shields decorated in individual fashion. Some of these have projecting bronze animals of fine workmanship which serve for defence as well as decoration. On their heads they wear bronze helmets which possess large projecting figures lending the appearance of enormous stature to the wearer. In some cases horns form one piece with the helmet while in other cases it is relief figures of the foreparts of birds or quadrupeds. Their trumpets again are of a peculiar barbaric kind; they blow into them and produce a harsh sound which suits the tumult of war. Some have iron breastplates of chain-mail, while others fight naked, and for them the breastplate given by nature suffices. Instead of the short sword they carry long swords held by iron or bronze chains and hanging along their right flank. Some wear gold-plated or silver-plated belts around their tunics. The spears which they brandish in battle, and which they call *lanciae*, have iron heads a cubit or more in length and a little less than two palms in breadth; for their swords are as long as the javelins of other peoples, and their javelins have points longer than swords.

All the elements of this remarkable description are supported by archaeological evidence and there is no reason to suppose that at least some of the Danebury warriors were not equally finely attired for battle.

Chariots

One vital element of the Celtic battle was the horse-drawn chariot. By Caesar's time chariot warfare had become obsolete in Gaul but when he crossed to Britain in 55 and 54 BC he found the traditional method of fighting still very much in evidence. He was so impressed that he spent some time explaining it in his war despatches for the benefit of the Roman audience:

> In chariot fighting the Britons begin by driving all over the field hurling javelins, and generally the terror inspired by the horses and the noise of the wheels is sufficient to throw their opponents' ranks into disorder. Then, after making their way between the squadrons of their own cavalry, they jump down from the chariots and engage on foot. In the meantime their charioteers retire a short distance from the battle and place the chariots in such a position that their masters, if hard pressed by numbers, have an easy means of retreat to their own lines. Thus they combine the mobility of cavalry with the staying-power of infantry; and by daily training and practice they attain such proficiency that even on a steep incline they are able to control the horses at full gallop, and to check and turn them in a moment. They can run along the chariot pole, stand on the yoke, and get back into the chariot as quick as lightning.

There can be no doubt from his description that as a fighting method charioteering could be highly efficient. The noise, vivid colour and movement would have suited the flamboyant Celtic temperament.

While Iron Age war chariots sometimes survive in graves in Yorkshire, and more widely in Europe, direct evidence is seldom found on settlement sites, but a number of cart or chariot fittings have been recovered from Danebury. In one pit the iron hoop bindings for the axle ends were found, while on the floor of one of the late houses a pair of linchpins came to light. These were used as a pin through the axles to prevent the wheels coming off. While these fittings *could* have come from chariots it is equally likely that they belonged to more mundane farm carts. However, on the floor of a large house just inside the east entrance, to the right of the main road, a set of bronze fittings belonging to an elaborate harness was found, including a very finely decorated strap junction, two button-link terminals and a terret ring (**31**). It was equipment of this kind that was probably used to deck out the ponies which pulled the war chariots.

If horses and chariots were as common in late Iron Age Britain as Caesar leads us to believe a legitimate question to ask is how many a community like Danebury may have possessed at any one time. It is an unanswerable question but it may not be irrelevant to point out that the entrance courtyard of the east gate would have made a convenient chariot park, while the protected kraal space around the fort could have provided adequate pasture for the ponies. The comparatively limited excavation at nearby Bury Hill produced a surprisingly large range of high quality horse gear (see **77**). That exceptional numbers of horse bones were also recorded raises the possibility that the community may have specialized in the manufacture of chariots and the breeding and training of pony teams. Alternatively the evidence might represent only a brief occupation of a warrior community at an exceptional time.

Warfare and raiding

By describing the defences and the weapons in this way, the impression may have been given that large-scale warfare was rampant. This was probably not the case; but that warfare was endemic seems highly likely. Celtic society in general was organized in such a way that warfare was an essential part of the system but quite often what ensued was aggressive

31 *Bronze horse harness fittings from the floor of building CS7/8.*

competition rather than outright mass slaughter. It was a means of establishing and reasserting social relationships at both an individual and a tribal level.

The classical writer Athenaeus provides an interesting insight when he says:

The Celts sometimes engage in single combat at dinner. Assembling in arms they engage in a mock battle – drill and mutual thrust and parry. But sometimes wounds are inflicted, and the irritation caused by this may lead even to the slaying of the opponent unless the bystanders hold them back . . . And in former times, when the hindquarters were served up, the bravest hero took the thigh piece, and if another man claimed it they stood up and fought in single combat to the death.

This, clearly, is the manner in which the nobility periodically tested their accepted social hierarchies. Any man who disagreed with the status assigned to him could contest it in full view of the assembled company.

Another test of status was the warrior's ability to encourage others to follow him in a raid. Raiding parties often followed the feast when a noble, wishing to enhance his standing, would encourage the others to join him in an expedition. In the cold sober light of the next morning anyone who dared opt out would be branded a coward. This is what Strabo was referring to when, having mentioned their love of war, he goes on to say:

When they are stirred up they assemble in their bands for battle quite openly and without forethought, so that they are easily handled by those who desire to outwit them. For at any time or place and on whatever pretext you stir them up you will have them ready to face danger even if they have nothing on their side but their own strength and courage.

The unstable equilibrium of society was, then, precariously maintained by relying on warfare as a self-adjusting system.

Warfare to a Celt was usually a short-lived affair, seldom likely to last more than a few days and more often than not over in a single day. It was only after Celtic society had come into direct contact with the classical world that more protracted conflicts became the norm.

If the prime function of early Celtic warfare was to establish the status of the individual and the tribe, its secondary functions were to maintain the tribal boundaries and to acquire booty. Tacitus, writing of the German tribes in the first century AD, is quite specific about the first point when he describes how it is considered appropriate for a tribe to maintain a depopulated zone around its borders. If this was a widespread phenomenon, it may eventually be possible to recognize tribal boundaries in the British archaeological record.

There is ample evidence in the classical writings to give a clear idea of how such a broader conflict might develop. After the preliminary skirmishings and demands had been made the two armies would assemble facing each other, the women, children and elders at the back of each, occupying the best vantage points. The first stage in the conflict was a war of words. Abuse would be hurled and wild boasts made by warriors driving their chariots up and down the enemy lines. As tempers rose each side would produce its champions to engage in single combat in front of the assembled company amid the clamour of screaming voices, the beating of shields and the raucous noise of the horns.

When the phase of single combat was over, either the assembled armies would accept the outcome and go home or the conflict would escalate into all out battle lasting until nightfall, by which time the result would probably have been decisive. Occasionally the armies would meet again next day but this was unusual. The conflict then was contained and governed by rules of procedure: it was more a visual demonstration of the strength of the tribe and the prowess of individuals than an attempt to decimate rivals. This type of conflict is widely known among primitive peoples: in our own society it has its counterpart in the football match.

The raid was rather different and a series of raids could be a prelude to a tribal conflict. Raids were organized by individual nobles against rival communities with the view to gaining booty, for distribution among those taking part. Quite often cattle were the target. The classic example in Irish literature is the *Táin Bó Cúailnge* or 'the cattle raid of Cooley', which begins as a cattle raid and ends in all out war. As one of the contestants says, 'every other combat and fight that ever I have made was to me but a game or a sport compared to the combat and the fight of Ferdia'. The story begins with Cú Chulainn's father calling the men of Ulster to battle with these emotive words, 'men are being killed, women are being captured and cattle are being driven'. As Cú Chulainn prepares for war against the men of Connacht his opponents offer two options – to release the noblewomen and the dry cattle; or the slavewomen and the milch cows – if he will

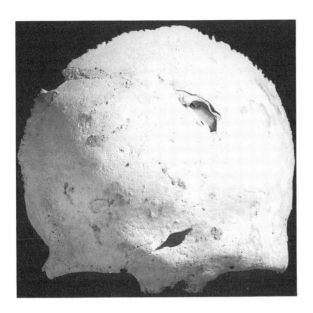

32a–b *Skulls with the marks of weapon blows.*

stop his raids, but negotiation comes to nothing and the conflict escalates.

Although the *Táin* was an Irish tale written down in the seventh century AD it reflects Celtic society largely unaffected by the presence of Rome and in many respects would have had similarities to the situation in southern Britain before about 100 BC – an effervescent

society, essentially unstable, and prone to conflict. There would presumably have been long periods of comparative peace culminating in periods of raiding, and these might have led to more prolonged aggression before society exhausted itself and fell once more into the lethargy of non-combat. The hillforts are the visible signs of just such a world. Danebury, with its sporadic bursts of defensive activity, signs of burning at the gates, charnel pits and ammunition dumps, is redolent of the uncertainties of the times. Embedded in its archaeological record is the story of the successes and reverses enjoyed by its inhabitants – the uncertain times of the sixth and fifth centuries, its rise to dominance about 350 BC, its centuries of pre-eminence and its final destruction about 100 BC.

The battles when they came were horrific affairs resulting in death and mutilation, now only dimly reflected in the archaeological record. Altogether the remains of more than 100 individuals have been found at Danebury. The deposits of bones represent a complex burial ritual which will be described later (pp. 103–8). A number show signs of severe injury (**32**). One particularly vivid case was of a man who had had a spear thrust into his forehead, the bone breaking away exactly to the shape of a spear in section; he had also suffered two other severe blows to the head. Another man aged 25–35 was struck in the centre of his forehead with a sharp-bladed weapon, probably a sword, but the weapon did not reach the brain and he recovered to live for weeks or even months after the assault. Another individual received a very heavy blow over his right eye, fracturing the eye socket and probably destroying or severely damaging the eye; he too lived on in a mutilated state. Several other skulls were found bearing evidence of sharp knife cuts of the kind that might have resulted from scalping. Straightforward descriptions of the injuries exhibited by the skeletal remains can do little to evoke the ever-present social horrors of endemic warfare. In considering next the physical surrounds of the occupants of Danebury and their daily lives, the background of stress against which the people lived should not be forgotten.

The settlement: its people and their homes

The defences of Danebury protected 5.3ha (13 acres) of the chalk hilltop where a sizeable community lived and worked in comparative security for almost 500 years. During this time they erected a variety of buildings and dug numerous pits into the chalk to serve as storage silos. Both activities peppered the surface of the hill with holes of all sizes – stake-holes 2cm (1in) wide, post-holes 20–80cm (9–34in) across, pits with diameters up to 2.5m (8ft) and irregular quarries averaging 10m (31ft) across. In all we estimate that there were about 4500 storage pits dug in Danebury and approximately 18,000 post-holes! At the end of each season's excavation, when all the features had been excavated, the surface of the chalk looked like a slab of Gruyère cheese.

Five hundred years of activity creates a confusing mass of detail but even a small-scale plan, showing all features undifferentiated by phase (**33**), emphasizes that a certain order and regularity remained effective throughout the history of the fort. Most obvious is the main road running across the centre between the two gates. Although no surface metalling survived it remained uncluttered by buildings throughout the period of occupation except at its western end when, following the blocking of the south-west gate, a few pits were allowed to encroach upon the now-defunct line. A narrow pathway branches from the main road and runs direct to the summit of the hill – an area which has not been excavated. Where it was leading is not known but the possibility that here lay a building of importance seems a reasonable hypothesis.

The other road lines are rather less clear, but two roads can be made out in the southern half of the site, running parallel with the rampart (**34**). Their lines are slightly blurred because the roads were laid out in the late period after the area had already been occupied for 150 years or so. Another road, metalled with tips of chalk, ran around the eastern periphery of the settlement at the inner edge of the quarry hollows behind the rampart, and there were traces of another parallel to it further towards the centre of the fort. Within this skeleton the settlement developed in the way we have already outlined.

Raw materials and tools for building
The raw materials used for building were all obtained locally. Most important was timber,

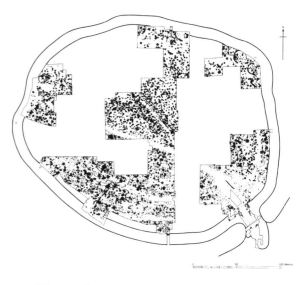

33 *Plan of the interior of Danebury showing all the Iron Age pits, post-holes and wall-slots discovered in the excavated areas. The plan represents 450 years of occupation.*

DANEBURY   SOUTH WEST SECTOR

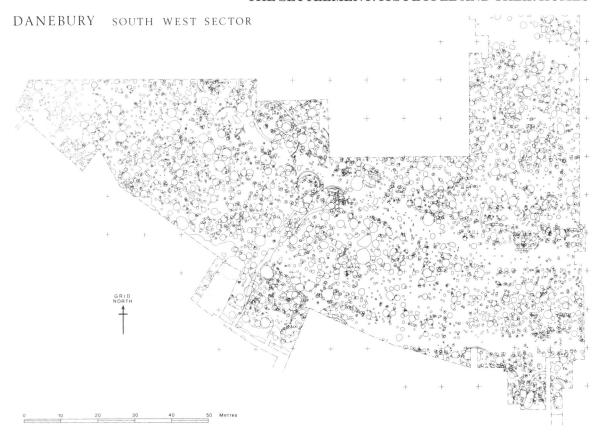

GRID
NORTH

0   10   20   30   40   50 Metres

34 *Plan of the south-west part of the site. The late period road lines can easily be distinguished. The circular trenches towards the centre are the wall trenches of early houses.*

oak being particularly favoured, no doubt for its qualities of durability. By the time that Danebury began to develop, much of the surrounding downland was already cleared for agriculture and pasture land, except for the steep hangers too difficult to plough. But not far away, both to the north and south, forests continued to flourish. About 8km (5 miles) to the north-east an extensive area of clay-with-flints caps the chalk downland flanking the river Test. This area, now Harewood Forest, seems to have been left unploughed in prehistoric times and would probably have supported extensive tracts of forest. Even larger expanses of clay, mixed with sands, are found about the same distance to the south on the edge of the Hampshire Basin. A wide variety of timber would have been available here in inexhaustible supplies, needing only labour to cut and cart it. Rather than drag entire trunks across

country to the fort, it seems far more reasonable to suppose that much of the rough work – the cutting, trimming, debarking, cleaving and seasoning – was carried out on the spot. Only when ready would the prepared timbers be transported. Whether the lumbering was carried out by gangs from the fort working in slack periods in the farming year or whether the communities living in the area produced timber for exchange we cannot hope to find out, but a number of small forts in the forest fringe, such as Holbury, Lockerley and Dunwood, may well have controlled the local timber supplies, providing seasoned timber in exchange for grain or wool.

Oak was used in a variety of ways at Danebury. Complete trunks up to 40cm (16in) in diameter were sometimes bedded vertically to form the main structural members of the 'granaries', but more often cleft trunks were used. The door-frames of houses often incorporated quartered timbers and at least one house had walls built of vertical planks split radially from a trunk 60–80cm (c. 30in) in diameter. The cleaving of timber, using iron or hardwood

55

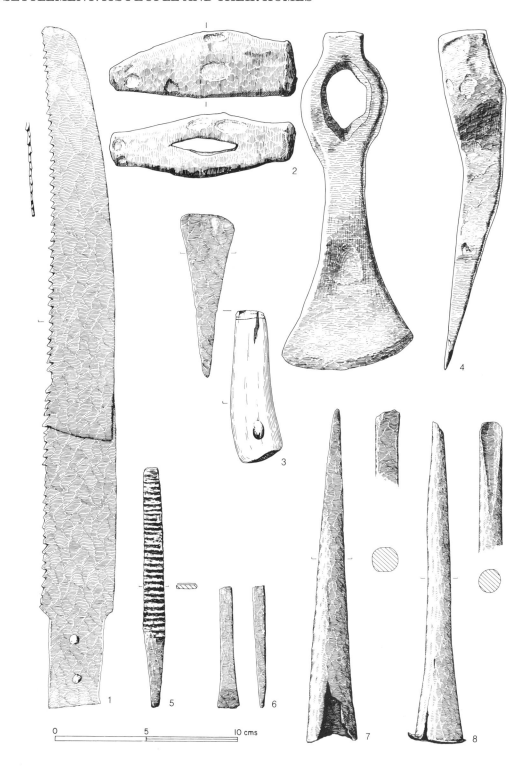

35 *Woodworking tools: 1 saw; 2 hammer; 3, 6
and 7 chisels; 4 adze; 5 file; 8 gouge.*

wedges, was an effective procedure which had the advantage of leaving a clean break much less susceptible to rotting than a sawn surface. A further advantage was that a cleft timber could more easily have had its sap wood removed leaving only the more resistant heart wood.

Another extensively used material was hazel, coppiced in such a way as to produce poles 1–3cm (½–1in) in diameter. These were used to make wattle walls and hurdles. It seems that two principal methods were employed, either the wattle was constructed as infill in pre-made wall frames, or, in the case of circular houses, the vertical poles were embedded directly in the soil along the desired wall line and the horizontals woven between them to form a continuous drum of wattlework broken only by its doorway. Wattle was widely used at Danebury. Since it was not a particularly durable material, a constant supply of coppiced hazel would have been needed but this could easily have been grown on patches of waste ground between the fields near the fort.

The working of timber on the site is well attested by a wide range of tools (35), the most important of which was the adze-hammer used for finishing the timbers and preparing simple joints. Small saws would also have been useful for the carpentry of more complex joints, for trimming wattles to length and for finer, non-structural woodworking. The occurrence of gouges with curved ends, effective tools for making circular holes, suggests that the pegging of joints may have been a regular practice. For preparing the wattles small sickle-shaped knives, which occur in some number, would probably have been used. Their form makes them ideal for deleafing the poles and splitting them where necessary.

Many of the wattle walls and wall panels would have been daubed with clay on the outside as a form of weatherproofing. Clay, often mixed with crushed chalk or chaff, was used to make ovens (36), hearths and small objects like loom weights. It was brought in from the Tertiary deposits of the Hampshire Basin and stockpiled until needed. Careful preparation was required which involved mixing in specially constructed conical pits, several of which have been found, all with squared flints on the bottom. The flints probably formed rests for the bases of the mixing poles to stand on. Clay and tempering were packed around

the pole together with plenty of water and the mixer walked around the pit holding the pole and varying the angle to stir the contents thoroughly. In this way both the consistency and composition of the daub could be controlled.

Another accessible, but essential, raw material was thatch for roofing. While corn straw could have been obtained in unlimited supply from the fields at harvest time it is more likely that reeds were used. These would have grown prolifically on the flood plain of the Test only 3km (2 miles) away, and could easily have been harvested by the inhabitants as and when they were required.

Building techniques

Thus all the necessities for making sound, comfortable buildings were readily to hand, and, in so far as we can judge from ground-plans and from tools, the constructional ability of the Iron Age inhabitants was considerable. There is no need to suppose that the structures were rustic hovels roughly lashed together. Efficient jointing and a complete mastery of materials would have meant stable structures finished to a high degree.

The principal house type at Danebury was a circular, one-door structure ranging between 6 and 9m (20 and 30ft) in diameter. About 70 have been excavated. They fall into two basic types: those built with walls of vertical planks bedded in continuous wall slots; and those whose walls were of wattlework.

Building CS1 is the only example of the first type (37–39). It had been built on an artificially created terrace cut into the chalk and for this reason had escaped the extensive erosion which has so denuded the other house plans, the only obscuring feature being a large tree which grew close to the doorway. The ground-plan consisted simply of a trench of circular plan, 20–30cm (9–12in) wide, cut into the chalk and continuous except at the door where two large post-pits were dug to contain the verticals of the door-frame. In the wall trench it was possible to distinguish two entirely different fillings: the soil-filled voids where the timbers had once been; and the chalk and flint packing on either side. Careful planning and dissection showed the wall timbers to have been individual planks up to 40cm (16in) in breadth placed end to end. That some of them were distinctly wedge-shaped showed that they had been split radially from a large trunk. This kind of wall

OVENS TYPE 1 & 2 Alternative arrangements

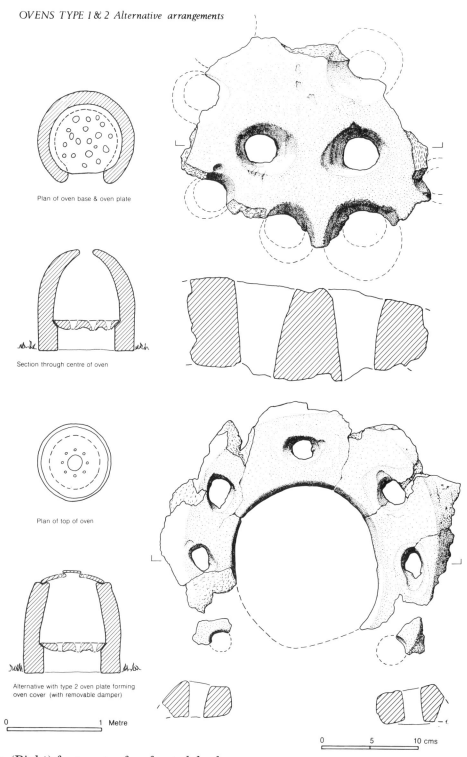

Plan of oven base & oven plate

Section through centre of oven

Plan of top of oven

Alternative with type 2 oven plate forming
oven cover (with removable damper)

0   1 Metre

0   5   10 cms

36 *Ovens. (Right) fragments of perforated daub
from oven plates. (Left) suggested alternative
reconstructions of ovens.*

CS 1

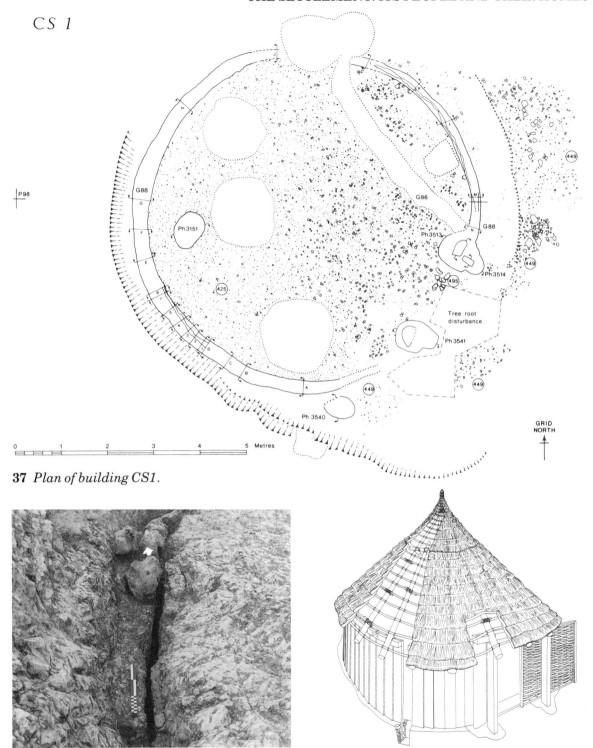

37 *Plan of building CS1.*

38 *Detail of the wall trench of CS1 showing the voids left after the vertical wall planks had rotted.*

39 *Tentative reconstruction of a plank-built house based on the plan of CS1 (drawn by Christina Unwin).*

construction would not have been particularly weatherproof but tongue and grooving, with moss and resin caulking, or more simply the attachment of additional planks to cover the joints, would have overcome problems of draughts and driving rain, while the possibility that the conical roof may have been taken down to the ground, providing additional insulation, has much to commend it.

The door-frame was constructed of two pairs of roughly squared timbers, one pair in line with the wall, the other in front and at right angles, creating a shallow porch-like structure. Both would have been kept rigid by lintels. Nothing survives to indicate what kind of door was provided but one possibility is that it was a movable wattle or plank structure which could be slotted into place between the pairs of vertical posts or removed altogether and kept inside when the house was open.

How the roof was treated can only be guessed, but a conical arrangement of rafters thatched with reeds would be simple and effective. The absence of internal supports might at first sight seem puzzling but so long as the wall top was suitably bound by a ring beam, the lateral thrust of the roof timbers would be contained and the whole structure would be quite stable.

The second type of house, similar to the first except that the wall was made of wattlework, was the most common type (**40–43**). A good example is provided by building CS20 where the details of the wattle wall are extremely well preserved (**40**). Here the individual vertical wattles, 2–4cm (¾–1½in) across, were driven into the ground at intervals of about 15cm (6in) around the circumference of the building. Driven, however, may not be quite accurate since it is probable that the holes were first made with a crowbar – a hard wood shaft with a pointed iron end – and the poles lightly hammered into place. Once in position the horizontal members could be woven to create a tough and comparatively rigid wall, quite strong enough to support the weight of the conical roof or to allow some of the verticals to be taken up to form a roof (**43**). The door-frame was much the same as that of the plank-built CS1 with two exceptions: first, there was an additional pair of posts in front, but since these were sealed by the chalk-rubble door-sill they may have been something to do with the building process, to be removed when the super-

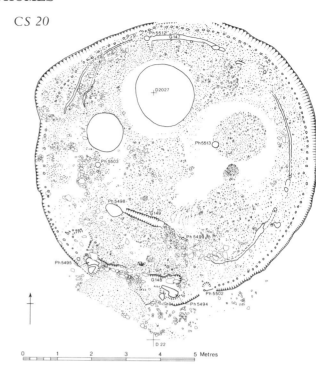

CS 20

40 *Plan of building CS20.*

structure was finished; second, a horizontal threshold beam had been laid between the posts of the inner door-frame. This is a particularly interesting feature to which we shall return again below.

Inside the building a rammed chalk floor survived but through it had been cut a shallow groove just inside the wall and not quite concentric with it. There was also an inner door-frame giving the impression, in plan, of being part of an inner vestibule. These features are unusual and not easy to explain, unless it is supposed that the inner slot took a slight wall of wattle to serve as an insulating inner skin and the vestibule was also part of an elaborate scheme to exclude the draughts. Another interesting feature was the two storage pits dug below the floor. Although they look rather hazardous on the plan, in their original form, before erosion, the mouths would have been little more than 50cm (18in) in diameter and could thus simply, and safely, have been closed by a board or wicker cover.

A number of buildings were discovered in which the only surviving traces of superstructure were the doorstops, the chalk door-sill and, where conditions of survival were good, the

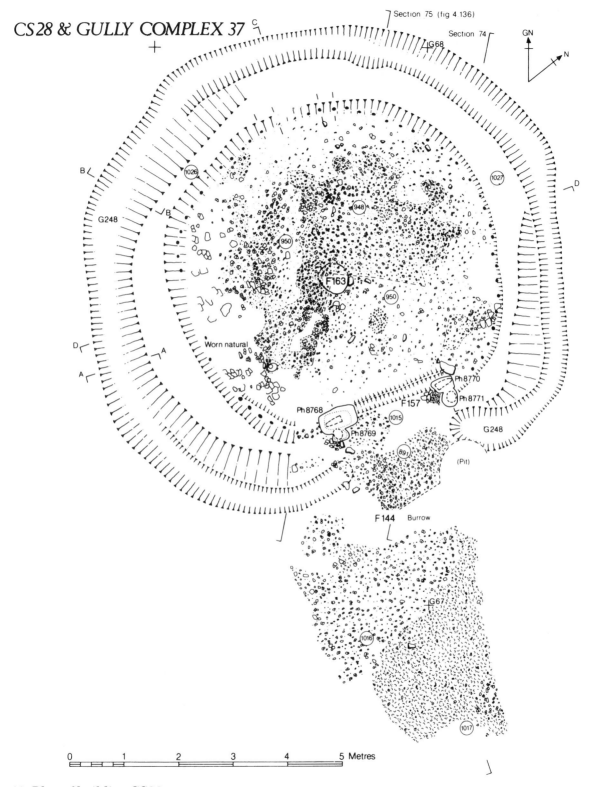

CS28 & GULLY COMPLEX 37

Section 75 (fig 4.136)

Section 74

GN

N

G68

1026

1027

B

D

G248

B

948

950

F163

950

D

A

A

Worn natural

Ph 8770

Ph 8771

Ph 8768

F157

Ph 8769

1015

G248

891

(Pit)

F144   Burrow

G67

1016

1017

0   1   2   3   4   5 Metres

41 *Plan of building CS28.*

42 *Building CS28 excavated. The door sill and doorposts lie just in front of the rod. The large irregular hole c.2m (6½ft) in front is a modern badger set.*

43 *Tentative reconstruction of a stake-built house based on the plan of CS20 (drawn by Christina Unwin).*

actual floor surface; there was no trace of wall timbers having been bedded in the subsoil. In other words the wall simply sat on the surface of the ground. One possible explanation for this is that the wattlework building had been constructed elsewhere and was physically moved to the new location. If this were so there would have been considerable advantage in the doorframe being kept rigid by a threshold braced between the lower ends of the frame posts, matching the lintel at the top. To site the structure would merely have required two new holes being dug for the projecting ends of the door-frame verticals.

Such an over-elaborate explanation needs to be further examined. In the first place why move a building? The answer to this must lie deep in the social structure of the community beyond archaeological reach; in the second, was it possible? In practice it is; a wattle wall could simply be uprooted or the stumps of the poles may already have rotted at ground level. If the thatch were removed a band of men could, without much effort, carry a small structure to a new location, where once sited, it could be rethatched. All this may seem far fetched but some such explanation is needed to contain the archaeological evidence. More to the point, the movement of timber structures is not unusual among surviving primitive communities.

The question of the superstructure of stake-built buildings presents interesting questions. Are we justified in interpreting the smaller stake-built structures in terms of wattle drum-like walls with conical raftered roofs? Another distinct possibility is that some of them may have been entirely of wattlework with selected wall poles bent inwards and bound in position with wattles to create a beehive style of roof continuous with the walls (see **43**). The exterior would certainly need to be thatched to weatherproof it but such a structure would be quick to build, strong, and easy to move. Raising this possibility, without offering a conclusion, shows something of the limitations of the archaeological data.

The use of different types of structure
So far it has been tacitly accepted that the circular buildings were all houses, but this need

44 *Excavations in the quarry hollow behind the rampart on the west side of the fort with building CS28 partially excavated in the foreground and another house stratified above it.*

not be so. The circular structures were quite suitable to house animals or farm equipment as well as people, and the range of interior fittings indicates a variety of different functions. Some of the buildings contained hearths or cooking ovens while others had storage pits dug beneath the floors, but none produced midden deposits or wear patterns suggestive of animals. On balance, then, a domestic use is likely, but ethnographic analogies show that in many societies the activities of a single family group are often divided between separate buildings: there may be a communal cooking hut, a weaving hut, a hut for wives and so on. The different internal fittings at Danebury might suggest that something of the kind was in operation here.

By far the best evidence for attempting to understand the changing structure of the community at Danebury comes from the deeply stratified deposits preserved immediately behind the rampart particularly in those areas where deep quarry hollows were dug to provide material for the rampart extension (rampart period 3). Here, not only are the structures well preserved but it is possible to separate out each of the successive occupational phases (**44**). The area behind the rampart on the east side of the

45 *Five-post structure (PS335) set within a circular drainage ditch.*

46 *Ring grooves for early circular houses in the south-west part of the site. The late road, still with some of its cobble metalling in position, can be seen in the foreground. Compare with 34.*

fort provides some of the best evidence of contemporary structures which is most easily summed up in phase diagrams based on the more detailed plans. In phase j1 most of the area was occupied by storage buildings but in phase j2 a series of houses was built. It looks very much as though buildings CS1 and CS2 together with the storage building, which cluster around an open area, were part of a single unit. In the next phase (phase k), buildings CS7 and CS55 were joined by a chalk metalled pathway with storage units between while in the final phase, phase l, two major buildings CS7/8 and CS54 appear to be the focal structures of discrete settlement units and are separated by an open area.

Further north, in the north-eastern corner of the fort, a situation of comparable complexity was discovered (**45**). The plans of phases j and k show how the settlement at this point developed within the basic residential structure, CS38 being rebuilt while the ancillary buildings were modified and extended.

The structural and sequential evidence of this kind, briefly touched on here, will, when fully assessed in relation to the scatters of artefacts found in the associated layers, be of enormous value in showing how the society worked and developed. This range of data from Danebury is unique in the British Isles.

So far only the building complexes of the late period have been considered, for the very good

reason that they are well preserved in deeply stratified contexts; but several clusters of early period buildings are known, one of which lies in the southern part of the fort excavated in 1979–80 (**46**). The arrangement here seems to suggest a row of circular houses, several of them showing more than one phase of rebuilding, arranged along a pathway, with a ditched enclosure on the opposite side. Unfortunately later pit digging has so destroyed the interior of the enclosure that it is difficult to tell what kind of building, if any, it may have contained but it is tempting to see it as a potential residence of high status, the rows of unenclosed buildings being subsidiary structures. This may sound rather fanciful but symbolic enclosure of a residence was a mark of status well-recognized in the Irish Celtic laws.

The size of the population at Danebury
The discussion of houses and of social groupings leads, naturally, to the extremely difficult question of population size. How many people actually lived in Danebury at any one time? The simple answer is that we do not know and can never know – at best we can offer inspired guesses. The issue of population estimates in general is one which has been widely discussed in the archaeological literature. Broadly speaking there are two approaches, both based on

empirical data derived from modern ethnological parallels. The first uses site area and offers the general formula that $P = 146\sqrt{A}$ where P is population and A is the total area of the settlement in hectares. Applying this formula the estimated population for Danebury would be 335 in any period. The second method uses the number and size of dwelling units arriving at the general equation: $P = A/10m^2$ where A is the total floor area of all contemporary dwelling units in square metres. This is more difficult to apply to Danebury for the obvious reason that we do not know how many houses there were and how many were in contemporary use, but

taking the latest phase, and assuming that the settlement as a whole is likely to conform in plan to that part which has been excavated, we arrive at the estimated number of houses being 53, with an average floor area of 38.5sq.m (414sq.ft) which, according to the formula, would give us a population estimate of 204. Both methods are, of course, based on a number of uncertainties and assumptions but since they are *different* assumptions the close conformity of the figures gives a limited degree of confidence. The best estimate we are able to make at present, therefore, is that in the latest phase the resident population could have been in the order of 200 to 350 and in the earlier periods it is unlikely to have exceeded this figure.

The function of post-built structures

The most commonly occurring structures, other than pits, in Danebury and indeed in Wessex settlements as a whole, are settings of four and six posts (less commonly five, seven and nine as well) arranged in a square or a rectangular plan (**47–49** and see **45**). The possible functions of these settings have been widely debated,

PS 196

GULLY COMPLEX 26 & PS347

47 *Plans of a four-post and six-post granary.*

48 *Reconstruction of a six-post granary* (drawn by Christina Unwin).

with suggestions ranging from granaries, houses and barracks for troops, to watch-towers and platforms for exposing the dead. The truth is that such a simple ground plan could allow a wide variety of reconstructions, permitting an equally wide variety of functions, and without additional evidence no firm conclusions can be reached from ground-plan alone.

The most widely held view is that the majority of these post-built structures were granaries. Buildings of similar plan, undoubtedly granaries, are found in late Iron Age to Migration period farmsteads in the Netherlands and western Germany and they recur throughout the folk architecture of much of Europe. In Finland and Romania, for example, granaries of this kind were in regular use into the early decades of this century and can still be seen in the countryside.

The basic structure is quite simple. The posts would stand to a height of about 1–1½m (3–5ft) above the ground surface to support a platform of joists upon which would be built the granary proper. A possible alternative would be to suppose that the posts stood the full height of the walls, the floor joists being attached to the verticals at the required height above ground. The desired effects were several: to isolate the body of the building from the ground to prevent rodents from getting in; to insulate the floor from damp; and to allow free circulation of air beneath in order to reduce the risk of combustion due to overheating. These were the principles adopted by the Romans when building military granaries and can be seen today embodied in the eighteenth- and nineteenth-century granaries, built on staddle stones, which still survive in many English farmyards.

The nature of the superstructure is not absolutely clear but for a society without nails the most effective method of construction would have been a panelled framework kept rigid by effective jointing, infilled with wattlework, daubed on the outside to waterproof it (see **48**). There is ample evidence, in the form of daub retaining the impression of wattle, to show that this technique was widely used at Danebury and the distribution of daub within the site concentrates in areas where the 'granaries' are densest. Roofing would presumably have been of reeds or straw.

Access to the raised floor would have been by removable ladder. The nature of the internal arrangements must be guesswork but a common arrangement in more recent examples is for the grain to be kept loose in bins built against the walls on either side of a narrow central gangway. There is no structural reason why such an arrangement should not have been employed in the Iron Age.

While this generalized description offers a reasonable interpretation of the more substantial four- and six-post settings with their massive posts, up to 60cm (2ft) across, it may not hold good for a distinctive group of slighter structures represented by settings of four posts, each of which seldom exceeds 20cm (8in) in diameter. These 'small four-posters' *could* have been of the form suggested above but they may have been rick platforms. Structures of this kind would have been very useful for a variety of purposes. Corn or barley, which had to be cut damp, could be stored in the ear and allowed to dry before threshing, or alternatively, if barley were cut green and stored, it would make admirable animal feed since the stalks would still be edible and nutritious. Another possibility is that leaf fodder in the form of branches cut in the spring or early summer, was stacked to be used as animal feed in the autumn and winter. Merely enumerating the possible uses is sufficient to underline our ignorance.

There is a significant chronological division between the small four-posters and the more substantial four- or six-posters at Danebury. Wherever the small four-posters have been found in direct relationship to pits, the timber structures can be shown to be earlier, even than pits containing pottery of ceramic phase 1/3. This implies that the small four-posters are among the earliest structures on the site and at least one example can be shown to pre-date the earliest rampart. The best examples occur to the north of the main road where 11 individual buildings were recognized arranged roughly in rows. Many others occur elsewhere in the fort

49 *A post structure partially exposed in the quarry hollow in 1977–8. In a subsequent excavation two more posts were found (below the bottom of the picture) showing that this was a rare example of a seven-post structure. At the top the mouth of pit 1115 can be seen with post-holes around.*

50 *One of the streets in the southern part of the hillfort showing rows of storage buildings, probably for grain (drawn by Karen Guffog).*

51 *Intercutting pits of various dates.*

but where features are particularly dense it is difficult to be confident about picking out convincing groups of four.

The rearrangement of the interior of the fort at the beginning of the late period saw a dramatic increase in the number of 'granaries' and it is probable that the vast majority, if not all, of the large four-, six- and nine-post structures belong to this period (see **50**). Most of them were laid out in well ordered rows arranged along streets which would have provided easy access for wheeled vehicles carrying products to be stored. The remetalling of the streets and the fact that the buildings were often reconstructed on the same spot is a clear

indication of continuity over a considerable period of time.

If all four-post structures are assumed to be granaries, then the only significant change between the early and late periods was in the solidity of the structures, and the fact that in the early period granaries were scattered in clumps throughout the site, whereas in the late period they were all concentrated in the southern part of the fort, occupying most of the available space. There would also therefore have been a considerable increase in storage capacity. If, however, the early, small four-post structures were fodder ricks then the change between the earliest and late period marks a dramatic reorientation in the economic system. These problems will be returned to later, in Chapter 7.

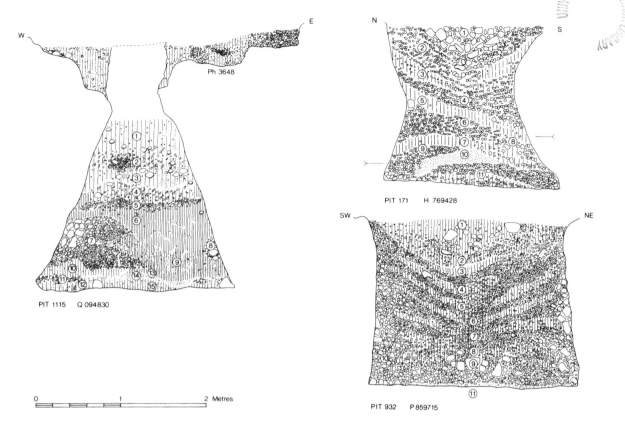

PIT 1115   Q 094830

PIT 171   H 769428

PIT 932   P 859715

0   1   2 Metres

52 *Three pit sections showing the silting patterns resulting from weathering of different intensities.*

Storage pits

Storage pits abound in Danebury: 2400 have been discovered during the excavation so far and we might expect another 2000 in the unexcavated area (**51–54**). The pits take a variety of shapes and sizes but fall into three basic categories: pits of circular plan; pits of subrectangular plan; and pits of conical profile. Of this third group only seven have been found and all showed signs of having been used for storing and mixing clay (see above, p. 57). The rectangular pits are comparatively rare, amounting to only about 7 per cent of the total; the majority belong to the early period. Three were found fitted neatly into an early house, CS9, preserved by the extension of the rampart on the north side of the fort, in a manner suggestive of their having been storage cellars. That the subrectangular pits were vertical sided would have made them unsuitable for the long-term storage of grain because they would

be difficult to seal, but other commodities could more easily have been stored in them.

The great majority of the pits were circular in plan and were of two sub-types: cylindrical pits with near vertical sides; and beehive pits with undercut sides causing the pit to widen out at the bottom. There were more than four times as many beehive pits, 72 per cent of the total, as there were cylindrical pits. Most of the pits had been left open after use and had become filled with a mixture of rubbish, together with silt and chalk eroding from the sides. In this process the upper part of the pit walls had usually crumbled away, completely altering the profiles, but a few, by virtue of their sheltered positions in the quarry hollows and very rapid filling, had preserved their profiles exactly as they were when originally dug. A very good example is pit 1115 (see **49** and **52**). It was nearly 3m (10ft) deep, 50cm (18in) wide at the mouth and 2.4m (8ft) wide at the base, with its walls and floors cut completely smooth. Even more interesting is the fact that the layers around the top of the pit were also well preserved. Chalk rubble had been piled up to form

69

53 *Adze marks on the bottom of a pit.*

a rim, the pit itself opening as a crater in the centre. More chalk rubble had been added to the rim during the life of the pit. One further detail of note is that several post-holes around the pit top could have supported a shelter over the opening.

All these arrangements may seem inexplicably over-elaborate until the question of how these pits are thought to have functioned is considered. The most likely explanation is that they were used to store threshed corn. The concept of tipping corn into a damp pit in the chalk might at first sight appear ill-advised but experiments have shown that it can be a highly effective method of storage so long as the top of the pit is provided with an airtight seal. What happens is that immediately the pit is sealed the grain in contact with the pit side begins to rot, a process which uses up the oxygen in the pit and gives off carbon dioxide. The percentage of carbon dioxide continues to increase to a point at which it kills off the bacteria and fungi causing the rotting and thus becomes self-sterilizing. From this point on the atmosphere is stable and the pit contents are safe from further disintegration until the airtight seal is broken. When the pit is opened, even a year after the original sealing, the mass of the grain will be quite fresh for consumption or for use as

seed, the only waste being a thin crust, 1–2cm (1in) thick, against the pit sides and bottom which, anyway, could be put to good use as cattle feed. The essential part of the scheme is the airtight seal: clearly the narrower the pit mouth the better. The beehive shape, therefore, is the result of the two prime requirements: a narrow pit mouth and a large volume. The advantage of the cone of chalk piled round the pit top is probably that it prevented the seepage of surface water and allowed a thickness of soil to be piled over the lid increasing the quality of the seal. The post-holes would have been useful to support a shelter against the weather at the crucial times when the pit was being filled and emptied. It is also possible that they anchored some kind of lifting gear.

For the most part the pits were dug with considerable skill with the aid of an iron adze, the marks of which are often still apparent on the pit walls and bottoms (**53**). Although the task seems daunting, it is estimated that two or three men working for a day could complete an average-sized pit with ease. The technique seems to have been to start the belling out immediately to increase working space, but as the pit deepened a pedestal of chalk was sometimes left undug presumably as an aid to passing out baskets of rubble: only later would it be finally removed. Evidence for all these stages is found in the small number of unfinished pits at Danebury.

With so many pits dug in such a restricted space over the 500 years or so of occupation it is inevitable that pit-diggers should sometimes break into old silted up pits long forgotten. Even if the new pit were begun in a surface of undisturbed chalk, by belling out it might soon encounter a neighbouring feature. Occasionally at this stage the new pit was abandoned but more often it was completed and the imperfect side made good with a wall of chalk blocks (**54**) or occasionally flints set in clay.

There were certain changes with time. It has already been noted that rectangular pits were restricted to the early period. The actual number of pits also declines but this does not mean that the pit storage capacity decreases in parallel because the average volume of the pits actually increases with time from 2.18 cubic m (77 cubic ft) in ceramic phase 1/3, to 4.35 cubic m (154 cubic ft) in ceramic phase 7–8. The implication of all this for the economy of the site will be considered in detail in Chapter 7.

54 *Blocking wall of chalk lumps built to revet the loose filling of the far pit into which the near pit was cut.*

The shrine

In the centre of the fort there is a group of four rather unusual rectangular buildings (**55** and **colour plate 9**). They face towards the entrance of the hillfort and are sited on the false summit of the hill, that is the area that appears to be on the skyline when viewed from the entrance but is in fact not the true crest. They are also aligned with the pathway running directly towards the main road and the east entrance. One of the buildings, RS1, lies astride the path and seems to have been some kind of fenced enclosure, quite possibly unroofed. All that can safely be said about it is that it is probably the latest of the group. The other three buildings were clustered together on either side of the path. Since all of them are related in some way to pits containing datable pottery (some pits are earlier than the buildings and some later) the buildings can be approximately phased. RS3 and 4 were probably laid out together first in the early or middle period of occupation while RS2 was added later, but the fact that its façade lines up with RS4 suggests that RS4 may still have been standing when RS2 was built.

All these buildings were probably constructed in the same way but the details are clearest in RS2 (**56** and **57**). The first stage of

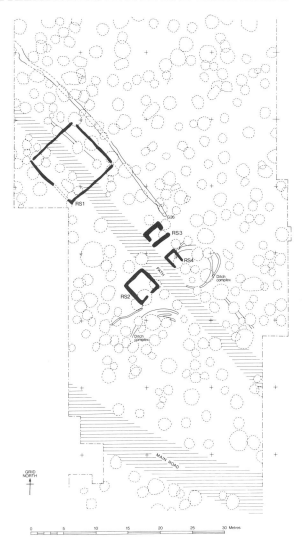

55 *General plan of the central area showing the four 'shrines'.*

the archaeological excavation entailed the very careful clearing of the surface of the filling of the wall trench, which had been cut into the chalk, and the top of two filled-up pits. The clearing showed two very distinct layers: a chalk rubble packing against the outside of the trench edge; and a far more soily band against the inside. When this stage of the excavation had been planned and photographed, the filling was carefully dissected leaving a number of vertical sections which were all drawn. The best preserved showed clearly that the difference in the fillings noted in the surface clearing also appeared in the vertical sections. The

56 *Building RS2 before and after excavation. Note how the wall slots had cut through the tops of filled-up earlier pits.*

simplest explanation for these observations is that the soil represents the position where the ends of thick timber planks had once stood, packed tightly into position by the chalk rubble. When the timbers had finally rotted, soil washed in to fill the voids thus created. If this interpretation is correct then we must imagine buildings with solid plank walls and presumably simple gabled roofs of reeds or thatch.

It is one thing to describe structures but another to explain their function. There is nothing associated with the Danebury buildings to give any indication as to how they were used, but the general type has turned up on Iron Age sites from time to time (**58**). At South Cadbury, for example, a not dissimilar structure was found in a prominent position at the end of a path lined with animal burials, suggesting to the excavator that it may have been a shrine. More recently a building of the general type has been found at Lancing, on a site later to be occupied by a Romano-British masonry-built temple, again emphasizing possible religious connotations. Even more dramatic was the discovery of a complex building at Heathrow. It looks very much like a combination of RS1 and RS2 from Danebury and in general plan is identical to a widespread type of Romano-British temple. Together, then,

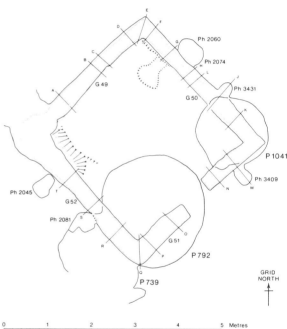

57 *Plan of building RS2 before excavation showing the soil filling the position once taken by the thick timber wall.*

the available evidence points to a religious use for these structures. Their dominant position in the centre of Danebury and the fact that at least one of these buildings was in use throughout much of the life of the fort adds further support to the hypothesis.

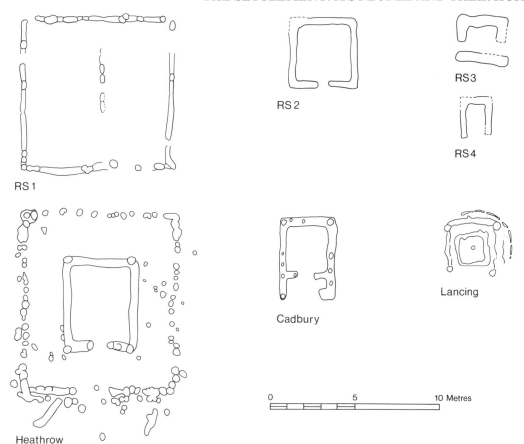

58 *Comparative plans of Iron Age shrines. RS1–RS4 are from Danebury. See also* **55**.

Conclusion

Having described the principal types of structure at Danebury it is necessary to stand back and take stock. Perhaps the most important general point to make is that there is much we can never know or understand. If there had been light buildings constructed of wattle that did not penetrate the subsoil nothing of their walls would survive. Similarly if the fort had been filled with buildings constructed on timber sills laid on the ground surface with wattle infilling there may well have been no trace except in the deeply stratified layers behind the ramparts where some indication might have been found. Another aspect of the same problem is the large number of post-holes recovered for which no structural purpose can be suggested. Some are clearly pairs which could have functioned as drying racks, hide stretching frames, looms, or any one of a host of other

uses. Others may have been little more than tethering posts while some may be parts of unrecognized and unrecognizable structures. In other words our picture is not complete nor can it ever be – every pit dug in, say, ceramic phase 7, could have destroyed part of an earlier building.

Recognizing that the structural data have limitations is a necessary constraint, not a cry of despair. There is much we can say even if there are some things we cannot. The overall picture is clear enough – an organized system of roads, houses clustering around the periphery of the enclosure, shrines in the centre and ample storage capacity in pits and granaries. All the structural elements of the settlement were short lived: by their very nature they had to be constantly replaced. But apart from the major reorganization about 350 BC, rebuilding and replacement seems to have been carried out within the strict limits of a controlled settlement plan and a stable socio-economic system.

7

Daily bread: the farming regime

All the food consumed within the fort and in the neighbouring farmsteads was produced in the immediate locality. Barley and wheat were the staple crops: protein came largely from milk, cheese and pork, augmented by beef, horse meat and mutton, which became available when beasts were slaughtered for reasons of culling or for feasts. Domestic chickens were also kept, probably for their eggs. Honey was the only available sweetener, while salt, imported from the south coast, was of importance as a preservative as well as an essential component of the diet. Dietary salt could also be obtained from blood: societies who find mineral salt hard to come by regularly bleed live cattle to provide for the needs of the community.

Field systems

The chalkland landscape was intensively utilized at this time, the Iron Age agricultural regime being the culmination of 3000 years of gradual experiment. By the end of the Iron Age, the landscape had been moulded and modified in a way which has left indelible marks. Although the countryside around Danebury has been subject to intensive modern ploughing it is surprising how much of the ancient agricultural landscape remains to be seen from the air. Photographed under the right conditions, when the corn is just ripening or after the fields have been ploughed and washed by the rain, it is possible to pick out cropmarks or soil marks representing the boundaries of ancient fields or the ditched and pitted enclosures of the contemporary farms. When these traces are plotted on a map the ancient landscape, in all its complexity, emerges, albeit in discontinuous patches where the visible evidence survives (**59**).

Since a map of these features reflects use over many generations the dating of the individual elements is not always possible with any degree of precision. Many of the field systems are in fact probably of Roman date, but sufficient evidence remains to enable some of the Iron Age components to be disentangled. The outer earthwork of Danebury, for example, gives way to a long linear ditch system which runs for more than a kilometre (½–1 mile) eastwards from the fort. About half way along the line, a limited excavation showed that it had become a pair of ditches, 7.5m (24½ft) apart, bounding what may well be a drove way. Further on, the air photographs show that the ditch system joins with another complex of trackways, running eastwards towards the valley of the river Test. Field boundaries extend outwards from these tracks in such a way as to demonstrate their contemporaneity. To the south of the southern track, on Longstock Down, there is a series of rectangular ditched enclosures, which, since they appear to have no internal features, could well be stock enclosures. Lying midway between the fort and the river, about 2km (1¼ miles) from each, they are well sited to serve as temporary kraals for animals being driven from the protection of the fort to the nearest water meadows. Another trackway, visible for almost a kilometre, runs southwards from an entrance in the outer earthwork. Adjacent to it and butting up to the earthwork traces of another field system can clearly be made out on the air photographs. It is evidence of this kind that enables some elements of the Iron Age landscape to be discerned.

In addition to trackways, fields and stock enclosures, it is often possible to recognize on air photographs the positions of the isolated

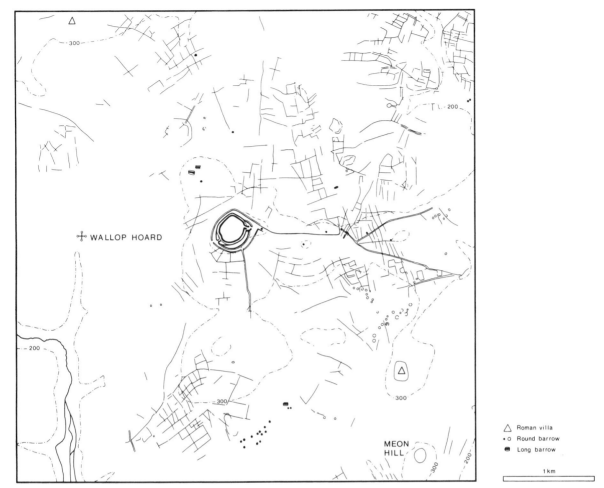

59 *Simplified plan of the Danebury region showing fields, trackways and enclosures and other ancient features visible on air photographs.*

farmsteads that were such an important element in the Iron Age socio-economic system. In the 40 or so square kilometres (*c.* 15 sq. miles) south of Danebury, in the valleys of the Test and its tributary the Wallop Brook, the evidence is particularly clear and we seem to have an almost complete pattern (**60**). Each farm is situated about one kilometre from its neighbour and all favour much the same kind of location on gently sloping spurs overlooking the river valley, between half and one kilometre from water. In this position they are optimally sited on good farm land with adequate accessible water for their cattle and not far from the higher chalklands where the sheep would be allowed to run. The impression given by the map is that the landscape was densely packed with isolated farms and that the land was being utilized to the full.

Agricultural tools
Agricultural technology was comparatively simple: the ground was broken with an ox-drawn ard, crops were sown by hand, and by hand, using a sickle, they were reaped. The ard was quite effective on light chalk soils but since it did not turn the soil (as a plough does) it seems that the fields may have been ploughed in two directions at right angles to break the soil sufficiently for sowing. Marks of cross ploughing are found frequently in Holland and Denmark and less often in Britain, though they do not prove that the fields were ploughed in two directions on the same occasion. If, however, cross ploughing was the norm, then the square plan of so many Celtic fields would be more easily understandable. Single direction

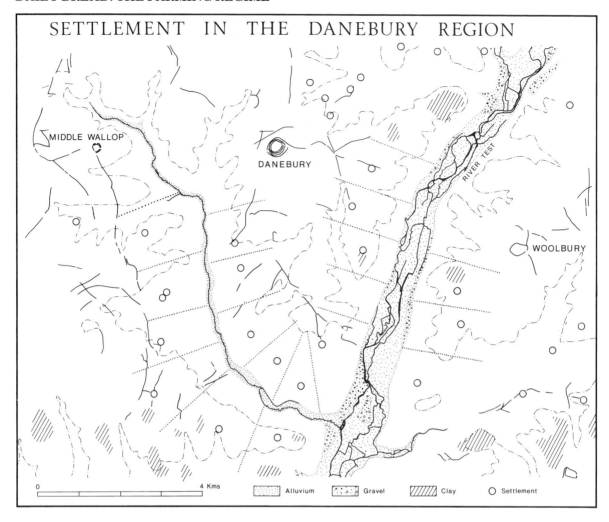

SETTLEMENT IN THE DANEBURY REGION

MIDDLE WALLOP

DANEBURY

RIVER TEST

WOOLBURY

0   4 Kms

Alluvium   Gravel   Clay   ○ Settlement

60 *Map of the Iron Age settlements revealed by aerial photography in the area around Danebury. Note the regularity of spacing. The dotted lines represent theoretical boundaries between different farms.*

ploughing tends to create long fields because of the natural desire to turn the plough as infrequently as possible.

The field boundaries, visible on the air photographs, were, until quite recently, evident as major banks, known as lynchets, caused by the gradual movement of soil down a slope to pile up at the bottom of the ploughed area. The process of bank-building would also have been accelerated when the flints were removed from the field surface and dumped at the edges. Some of the lynchet banks reached considerable proportions but this was very much to the

benefit of the farmers: the more massive the downhill lynchet became the less the field sloped, but more important was that the lynchet itself often embodied a depth of soil which encouraged growth. Thus while the uphill part of the field, where the plough bit into the chalk, was comparatively infertile, the lower, lyncheted part could be relied upon to produce a good crop. A further advantage was that the lynchet slopes could be encouraged to grow trees and undergrowth providing fire wood and coppice timber for building, in much the same way as the bocage of Normandy and Brittany is cropped in recent times.

The ard itself and its harnessing arrangements seldom survive except in waterlogged conditions, but quite often the tip of the ard was strengthened with an iron shoe or an iron point (**61** and **62**). Several ard shoes have been found

61 *Reconstruction of a typical Iron Age ard.*

at Danebury together with a thick iron bar, worn at the end, which is probably a bar share of the kind that would be attached to the wooden share and gradually driven down as the projecting point wore away.

The crops

The crops themselves are well represented in the pit fillings in the form of carbonized grains, recovered when the soil samples are subjected to a process of flotation (**63**). The most popular crops were spelt wheat (*Triticum spelta*) and hulled six-row barley (*Hordeum polystichum*), both of which were winter-sown varieties. Winter sowing was a great advantage because if some of the fields were planted after autumn ploughing the crop would grow and ripen early in the harvest season, ensuring a supply of fresh grain at a time when stored supplies may have been running low, as well as spreading the labour-intensive process of harvesting.

The crops were grown on a variety of soils. This became clear when weed seeds found with the cereal grains were identified (**64**). About 40 different species were recorded, the majority of which were quite usual in chalkland fields but a few were specific to quite different environments. Two plants, creeping scirpus (*Eleocharis palustris*) and a sedge (*Carex sp.*) show that damp ground of the kind found along the river banks was being cultivated, while two others, sheep's sorrel (*Rumex acetosella*) and corn marigold (*Chrysanthemum segetum*) are intolerant of chalk but are associated with acid soils like the clay-with-flints which caps the chalk downs to the north of Danebury.

The crops were cut using a small iron sickle (**65**), but it is difficult to be sure if the cutting included the straw or simply the heads. The presence of certain short stemmed weeds suggests that in some cases the straw was cut low but this need not have been invariably the case and there is increasing evidence to show that cropping regimes were both complex and varied. In some cases the grain seems to have

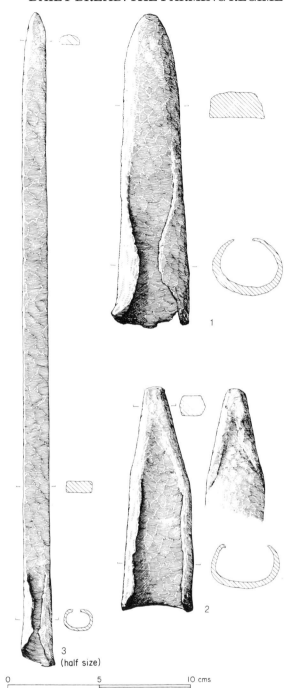

3
(half size)

0   5   10 cms

62 *Iron ard tips and a bar share.*

been stored in the ear but more often it was threshed before being tipped into pits or shovelled into granaries. The analysis of the Danebury samples suggests that grain was being brought to the site either already

77

63 *Charred grains of wheat and barley from pits at Danebury.*

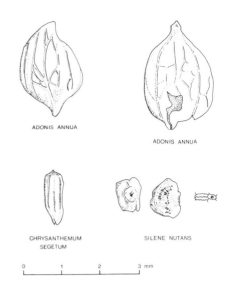

ADONIS ANNUA

ADONIS ANNUA

CHRYSANTHEMUM SEGETUM

SILENE NUTANS

0   1   2   3 mm

64 *Weed seeds brought in with the grain to Danebury* (drawn by Martin Jones).

threshed or in the ear ready for threshing, the straw having been removed beforehand. This raises very interesting questions about the social status of the fort and goes some way to supporting the view that some at least of the grain may have come from neighbouring farms where the initial stages of preparation had already been accomplished.

Once inside the fort the harvest went through various processes of cleaning, threshing, winnowing and storage. It would then have been divided into three components: grain for human consumption; seed; and animal feed. The animal feed has tentatively been identified at Danebury as barley mixed with large quantities of waste products derived from cleaning and threshing. We should not, however, overlook the possibility, discussed above (p. 67), that barley was also cut in its unripe state and stored complete with straw, on rick stands, to be fed whole to animals as required. Stacks of this kind, suitably fenced, could have been left in the fields or paddocks to provide a handy supply of winter feed.

Grain storage

Whether or not seed corn and consumption corn were separately treated is not clear. It used to be thought that seed corn was stored in above-ground granaries and the consumption corn in pits, but after experiments showed how important it was for the pits to be kept sealed if the contents were to stay fresh, the argument was reversed on the grounds that once the pit seal had been broken it was necessary to use all the grain immediately and the volume was so great that it could not be eaten fast enough. The argument was superficially attractive – the average Danebury pit could feed six people for a year – but when considered more carefully it need not hold good. There is no reason, for example, why a single pit should not be a communal store belonging to an extended family or kin group. If so it is possible to envisage an opening followed immediately by the distribution of the entire contents to all members of the group who would keep their share for shorter periods in baskets or leather sacks. Another alternative is that once opened, the contents of a pit may have been decanted to a granary for gradual distribution. This suggestion could take with it the further possibility that all grain was stored in pits and only the consumption grain was moved to above-ground stores when necessary. Which of the many possibilities approximates to the true situation will never be known, but simply listing a few of

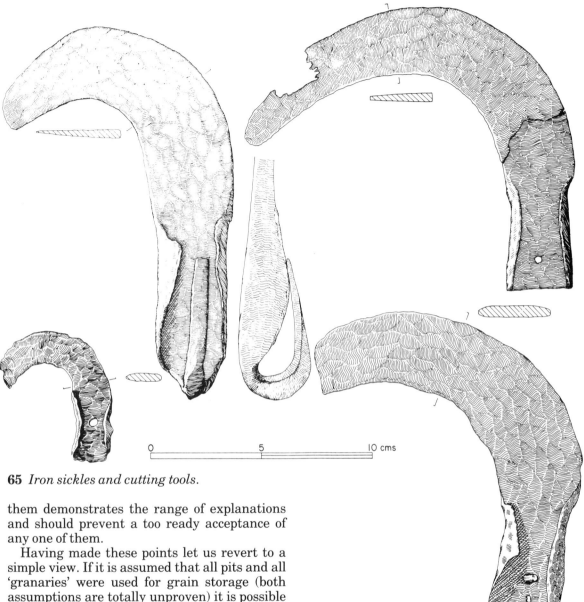

65 *Iron sickles and cutting tools.*

them demonstrates the range of explanations and should prevent a too ready acceptance of any one of them.

Having made these points let us revert to a simple view. If it is assumed that all pits and all 'granaries' were used for grain storage (both assumptions are totally unproven) it is possible to begin to approach the problem of storage capacity both in relative and in absolute terms. Comparing Danebury with normal settlement sites, likely to be the farmsteads of extended family groups, it can be shown that the pit storage capacity, area by area, at Danebury was about five times that of the typical farmstead, and since Danebury averages about four times the area of the farmsteads the total pit storage capacity of Danebury is twenty times greater. To go further with the statistics is impossible since there are two principal unknowns: the number of years a storage pit could be used and how many of the so-called granaries were used for corn storage. Since there is no way these questions can be resolved it is pointless to attempt to work out potential storage capacity (the question of the pits will be returned to in another context later, pp. 100–3). All that can safely be said is that the storage capacity at Danebury remained more or less constant throughout the life of the settlement.

There is ample evidence to show that a

66 *Pair of quernstones discarded in the filling of a pit.*

percentage of the consumption grain was ground on hand mills (or quernstones) to make flour (**66** and **67**), while the presence of small ovens is a reminder of the importance of baking. Barley could also be used to make beer but no archaeological evidence of brewing survives. Given a predominantly cereal diet, figures have been calculated which suggest that 1 cu.m (35 cu.ft) of grain will provide sufficient food for two individuals for a year. The storage potential of the granaries alone would have been greatly in excess of the needs of the resident population.

Animal husbandry
Any assessment of animal husbandry must be based largely upon the analysis of animal bones found in archaeological contexts on the site. In the first ten years of excavation nearly a quarter of a million individual fragments were recovered constituting the largest sample so far extracted from any single prehistoric site in Britain. When it is remembered that each fragment has to be washed, marked, identified and measured, and that all these details, together

with observations on butchery techniques and disease, have to be recorded in a computer-ready form, something of the task involved can be appreciated. The sorting of all this data can be carried out only with the aid of a computer.

The animals represented were sheep, goat, cattle, pig, horse, dog, cat, red deer, roe deer, fox and badger. There were also fish and a number of different species of bird. As **Table 3** shows, the relative percentages of the different species varied considerably.

There are various methods used to assess the relative frequency of animals present. The figures above are based on a counting of the total number of fragments identifiable. Another method, often favoured, counts only the epiphyses (the articular ends of bones) but the percentages derived in this way are almost identical to those above. A third method assesses the minimum number of individuals present in the sample but again the figures are not significantly different.

Several interesting general points emerge, the most evident being the consistency of the percentages through the entire life of the hillfort. From the evidence of the bone refuse it seems that there was little significant change in animal husbandry in 500 years of occupa-

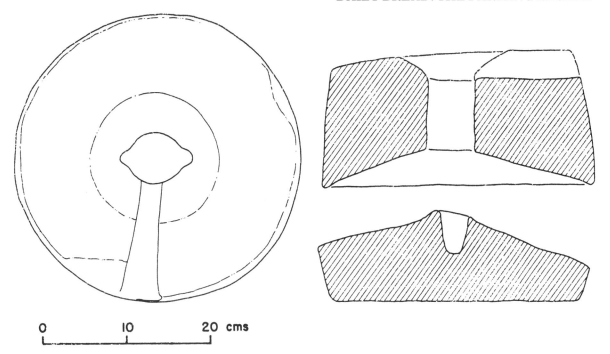

```
0          10          20 cms
```

67 *Drawing of the top and bottom stones of the quern in* **66**. *A handle would have been fitted into the slot in the upper surface of the top stone. A wooden pivot in the centre was small enough to allow corn to trickle down from the hopper in the top stone.*

tion. Since much the same point can be made of the crops there must have been a considerable degree of stability in the farming regime. Another general observation is the predominance of sheep throughout. This does not, however, mean that the diet was dominated by mutton. A single Iron Age sheep carcass produced only 14 per cent of the meat of a cow. A pig would have contributed nearly twice as much as a sheep. Readjusting the figures for the early period for actual meat yield the figures become cattle 67 per cent, sheep 23 per cent, pig 10 per cent. Another point which should always be borne in mind when dealing with figures of this kind is that they reflect nothing more than the carcasses that, for a variety of reasons, ended up in the fort. They do

Table 3 Percentages of animal bones found at Danebury

	Early	*Middle*	*Late(a)*	*Late(b)*
Sheep/goat	56	57	58	66
Cattle	23	16	16	21
Pig	15	18	14	8
Dog	1	2	6	2
Horse	1	4	3	3
Red deer	x	x	x	x
Roe deer	x	x	x	x
Bird	2	1	3	x
Cat	x	1	x	x
Fox	1	x	x	x
Badger	x	x	x	x
Fish	x	x	x	x

Note: x means less than 1 per cent. The late period is divided into two: a) is equivalent to cp 6, b) is equivalent to cp 7 + 8 (see **Table 2**).

68 *Reconstructions of typical Iron Age sheep and cattle based on the nearest surviving modern breeds* (drawn by Mike Rouillard).

not necessarily represent the actual flock and herd compositions. There are more complex factors involved which can only begin to be appreciated when the age profiles, breed variations and nutritional standards of the animal population are considered in detail.

The Danebury sheep were slender, horned, beasts rather like the Soay sheep found today on the Scottish island of St Kilda (**68**). They were probably fairly hairy and shed their coat annually in a spring moult. This would have meant that, instead of shearing, they could more easily have been plucked, perhaps using the bone combs which are so frequently found on Iron Age sites.

A study of the age at death of the Danebury flocks showed that a very high percentage of those found in the fort died young. About a third died in the first year of life and as many as a half were under eighteen months old. A considerable number of neonatal lambs were also found. Together this evidence strongly suggests that pregnant ewes were probably

rounded up in spring and brought in from the downs to the protection of the fort. While they could have been kept in the main enclosure, the outer enclosures, created by the middle and outer earthworks, were admirably designed to protect the lambing pens. Stores of supplementary food would have been on hand particularly as it was at about this time in the year that the food storage pits were being emptied providing nutritious scrapings and residues for the animals. The other great advantage of having the ewes close at hand, at the time when grain supplies may have begun to run low, was that with a high lamb mortality rate there would have been a surfeit of milk for the inhabitants of the fort.

Flock maintenance was of crucial importance to the community. A ewe does not lamb until her second or third year and with fertility sometimes as low as 60 per cent and neonatal loss high, it may not always have been easy to keep up the number of breeding females. Care at lambing times was therefore vital.

A study of the tooth eruption sequence has enabled the age at kill to be assessed and this in turn tells us about the management of the flock (**69**). For example, very few sheep seem to have been killed at the time when they would have been at their best for meat but there is a peak of killing at about a year old, probably after the beasts had been fattened on spring grass. These were most likely the young males surplus to the well-being of the flock: in medieval times only one ram was needed to serve 30–35 ewes.

About a third of the Danebury sheep were mature animals, well past the optimum age for meat production. These were probably breeding ewes and others kept for their wool. They would have been allowed to live for as long as they had an economic value and were productive; culling came in old age as they degenerated. Significantly, a high percentage of the old sheep found at Danebury suffered from peridontal disease – a disease of the mouth which prevents them from eating properly. It is just this kind of sickly animal that would have been picked out and killed. The carcasses were not wasted: as butchery marks on the bones show, they were cut up for food.

The flocks, then, were maintained essentially for wool production, and meat and milk were little more than useful by-products resulting from careful management. There is also ample

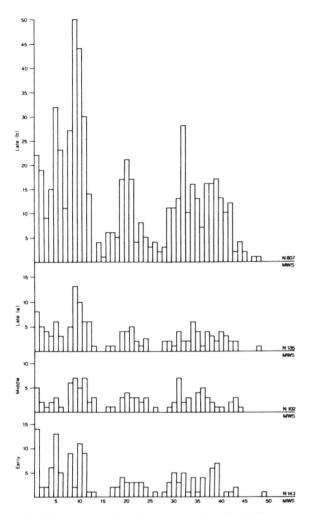

69 *Histograms showing age at death of sheep in each of the four periods. The relative age of the animals is given in the vertical scale* (compiled by Annie Grant).

evidence to show how significant wool was to the economy but this will be considered more fully in the next chapter. Another crucial by-product of sheep rearing was their manure. Since chalkland soils are comparatively thin and of only moderate quality, if fields were not regularly manured constant cropping would have led, eventually, to soil exhaustion. The great advantage of sheep is that, not only is their manure of high quality, but they can also be left to roam the upland fields for long periods at a time without being taken to water. There is, therefore, a close relationship between arable and sheep: if upland arable were to be extended to produce more grain, flocks would

have to increase in proportion to provide manure and this in turn would lead to an increase in wool production.

So far, only sheep have been considered, but the percentages for sheep quoted above also include some goats because it is frequently not possible to distinguish between the bones of the two animals. However, if the horn cores are examined (and these *are* distinctive) then the number of goats appears to be very small, only 2 per cent of the sheep/goat total in the early and middle periods and less than 1 per cent in the later phases. This is not surprising since goats are more difficult to manage but a few tethered about the fort would have provided a useful supply of milk and cheese.

Judging from the surviving bone sample, cattle seem to have been kept in much smaller numbers than sheep. This, to some extent, was determined by the environment: cattle need regular access to large supplies of water (a modern Friesian in milk may drink 45–53 litres (12–14 gallons) a day) and require much higher quality pasture than sheep. The chalk down-land is, therefore, not suited to large-scale cattle production but the river valleys, especially the Test with its wide fertile water meadows, could support considerable herds. The cattle eaten at Danebury would have spent much of their lives in the valleys and on the valley slopes.

The relatively large number of very young calves in the Danebury samples suggest that, like lambing, calving was carried out in or close to the fort where pregnant cows could be looked after during winter and given supplementary feeding. This would have required the storage of very large quantities of food stuffs in the form of hay or leaf fodder, collected in the spring and early summer. The annexes around the fort could have been used for this purpose but it is also quite possible that other specially constructed compounds spread around the countryside were used for calving. The rectan-gular enclosures which lie on the trackway between Danebury and the river valley (above p. 74) are ideally suited. Hay from the water meadows and leafy branches cut from the hangers and lynchet slopes during early summer could easily be stockpiled here and, if danger threatened, the fort was only 2km (just over a mile) away along the drove way.

No evidence was found that young cattle were killed when they were at their best for eating. The majority of the bones were of mature and old animals suggesting that only those diseased or barren were slaughtered for food. The herd probably consisted of fertile cows for breeding and oxen for pulling ploughs and carts (castrated to ensure docility) together with a few bulls to serve the cows.

The importance of cows, in some Celtic societies, lay in their value as a ready form of wealth which could be displayed, traded or invested. Some Irish law tracts reflecting Celtic society of the early first millennium AD, show how cattle-owning nobles lent their beasts to clients in return for goods and services. (These issues will be considered more fully in Chapter 9.) In such a system the principal value of a cow lay in her breeding capacity, but in addition she provided milk for short periods during the year, blood when needed and manure for the fields. Once an old beast had reached the end of its useful life its carcass would yield meat, sinew, horn, bone and hide – all extremely valuable commodities. That the Greek geographer Strabo, writing of the exports of late Iron Age Britain, specifically mentions hides, is an indication of their commercial value, but a value greatly enhanced in his time by the needs of the Roman army in Gaul and the Rhine provinces. Before Caesar's conquest of Gaul in the middle of the first century BC such hides as were produced would have been largely for local consumption.

Although pigs were not particularly numerous at Danebury, they are very useful animals. They can live almost anywhere, though they prefer woodland environments, and since they are omniverous they can be fed with waste left over from the diet of humans. To make maximum use of the herds, in complement to the needs of the other animals, they would have been turned into the woodland to forage in autumn and winter, spending the spring and summer in rough pastures or areas of heath. In the later summer and early autumn after harvest they would be set loose in the fields, after the cattle and sheep had gathered what they could, to root out the last goodness from the stubble. In other words they were excellent scavengers and could turn a wide range of almost inedible waste into top-quality protein. In addition to this, pig manure is of the highest quality.

The only constraints on pig breeding were that a large enough female population had to be maintained to keep the size of the herd at the required level, but since a sow will produce two litters of five or six piglets each year, this can have posed little problem. Thereafter animals could be killed as and when they were required for food. The ease with which sides of bacon can be smoked or salted means that most families would have been able to store surplus meat throughout the year, though the animal bones suggest that young sucking pig was also a popular meal.

Horses and dogs contributed significantly to the economy but were far less frequently represented in the bone assemblage than were the three principal meat animals. Horse represented only 3 per cent of the bones recovered from Danebury. There were other differences too. The total absence of bones of young foals shows that breeding took place elsewhere. This situation can be paralleled on other sites and it has been suggested that horses were not carefully bred at all during the Iron Age but were periodically rounded up, the two- to three-year-old males being selected for breaking in and training to become pack animals, riding mounts and chariot teams. This would also explain why the great majority of the Danebury horses were male, since the mares would be left to run with the herd. In the late period, however, there were signs of a change: some bones of young horses are found, one of which was under fifteen months. It is tempting to see this as evidence of a change towards a more controlled system of stock management. The very high percentages of horse found at Bury Hill towards the end of the late period is a further indication of the changes now underway.

At the end of their useful life old horses may have been killed for food. At any event, their bones show signs of butchery. While there is no difficulty in supposing that horse meat was eaten by the inhabitants it could just as well have been fed to the pigs or the dogs.

Dogs were present, though in comparatively small numbers. A range of sizes is indicated, but we cannot say whether animals were carefully bred to perform specific functions. Of most use would have been sheep-dogs and dogs suitable for herding cattle, but Strabo lists hunting dogs among the exports from Britain. While hunting may indeed have been a sport enjoyed by the occupants of Danebury the dearth of wild animal bones in the fort shows that prey was not brought back for consumption on site. The forests no doubt abounded with both red deer and roe deer but the total number of deer bones found at Danebury could be accounted for as the remains of no more than five individuals. Clearly, then, venison was not consumed in any quantity in the fort but shed antlers were collected as a useful raw material for the manufacture of tools and ornaments.

The dogs living around the site need not all have been useful. Some may have been scavengers, others were perhaps pets. The same may be said of cats whose presence is attested in all periods. The only difference between wild and domesticated cats lies in their size which is not always a reliable guide, but the fact that many of the Danebury felines were young, and one was a small kitten, strongly suggests that they were domestic. As such they would have served a useful purpose in keeping down vermin.

Among the other animals found can be listed badger, fox, hare, mole, weasel, wood mouse, yellow-necked mouse, house mouse, water vole and short-tailed vole. None are particularly surprising. Fox and badger could have been hunted or trapped for their fur, the yellow-necked mouse and house mouse are typical pests where grain is stored, while some of the vole bones might have been introduced in the pellets of birds of prey. None were of economic significance but together they enliven our picture of the community.

Bird bones were found in all periods, presenting an interesting range of species. Domestic fowl was present but only in the latest layers. This conforms with evidence from elsewhere in southern Britain which suggests that fowls originated in the East and spread throughout Europe in the Iron Age, reaching Britain no earlier than the second century BC. Among the wild game birds represented geese and swan are found, but the exact species are not easily identifiable. Ducks of various types were recognized, including mallard, widgeon, teal and goosander. Other possible game birds include grey heron, black grouse, quail, corncrake, golden plover and kittiwake. The kittiwake is particularly interesting since it is a coastal bird of restricted range, which still breeds on the coasts of Dorset and the Isle of Wight. It is difficult to see how it could have got inland as far as Danebury unless it was brought in, perhaps as a delicacy.

All the birds mentioned above could have been brought to the site to eat (though there is little evidence that they were eaten). The rest of the list were probably killed or died around the site; perhaps they were picked off during bouts of sling practice! They include birds of prey such as buzzard, red kite, kestrel and peregrine falcon and many others: wood pigeon, sky lark, wagtail, redwing, song thrush, shrike, house sparrow, starling, raven, jay, jackdaw, rook and crow. Ravens occur in surprisingly large numbers (11 in the early period, two in the middle period and eight in the late period). One reason may be that the number reflects little more than the availability of rubbish dumps and carrion for them to feed off but since the raven is a bird of some importance in Celtic mythology its presence at Danebury in such numbers may have a deeper significance.

The list of mammals and birds represented by their skeletal remains in the Danebury rubbish deposits is a long one but its length should not obscure the overriding importance of the three basic farm animals – sheep, cattle and pigs – to the well being of the community. The care of the flocks and herds, and in particular the maintenance of a healthy breeding stock, was a matter of life and death. Animal husbandry will have absorbed a considerable proportion of society's labour.

Agricultural systems

Animal husbandry and crop production have been discussed separately but to give the impression that they were independent would be quite wrong – they were inextricably bound up in a single stable system of food production in which each component was carefully balanced with, and complementary to, all the others.

The emphasis was on the production of grain for human consumption. The diet was largely cereal and by focusing at this end of the energy-fixing chain the community was making maximum use of the available resources. (The conversion of grain to animal protein for consumption is a very wasteful procedure.) If then the prime concern was grain production what part did animal husbandry play? Why bother with the time-consuming raising of stock? There were probably many reasons, among which dietary variation would have loomed large, but the principal concern was to diversify the potential food base by storing surplus as live protein. To put this in practical terms, the land could produce plant products unacceptable to man as a food – grass, leaves, acorns etc. – while crop-growing and processing regimes yielded waste products such as straw, grain spilled in the fields during harvest, threshing and winnowing waste, partially fermented grain from the sides of storage pits and so on. All this could be turned to productive purposes by feeding it to animals. In this way waste carbohydrate was converted into an easily maintained and readily accessible store of protein and fat.

The flocks and herds can be seen in much the same way – as a food supply that could, through careful curation, be made to yield calories for humans when needed, together with a range of 'waste' products that could be used as raw materials, to provide sustenance for other beasts, and manure for the fields. In the spring breeding season the culling of unwanted new-born, together with neonatal deaths, produced a surfeit of protein for immediate consumption by humans in the form of meat and milk, and for storage as cheese and by feeding to the omniverous pigs. Nothing was wasted. Subsequent cullings and natural deaths fed humans and pigs and provided useful materials for manufacturing processes. The pig was of vital importance in eating all the detritus of butchery rejected by man.

The overall aim was to maintain the flocks and herds at the optimum level, but the sheep and cattle represented not only a store of protein in times of need but a measure of society's wealth. Cattle were a readily exchangeable commodity while sheep regularly produced wool which could be spun and woven into finished products for storage or exchange. In other words the flocks and herds could be made to yield surplus for large-scale exchange.

The discussion so far has tended to regard the system as stable but this need not have been so. In 500 years some change is only to be expected but this is surprisingly difficult to recognize in the faunal and floral remains from the site. Indeed, as has been discussed, the animal bone analysis suggests a remarkable uniformity and this is also supported by the results of the sampling procedures used to study the plant remains. If, however, the animal bone assemblages from sites on the chalkland pre-dating Danebury are examined, a more fluid situation in which comparatively high percentages of cattle decline as sheep

increase is evident. On present evidence then it seems that the first half of the first millennium was a period of change and that by c. 500 BC a stable regime had been developed, in which sheep rearing predominated.

The reasons why such an orientation should have taken place were, no doubt, complex, but one possible model has much to offer. If the population was increasing throughout this time, as seems quite likely on a variety of evidence, there would have been an increased pressure on land suitable for crop production which would have led to over-cropping and decline in fertility in the traditional agricultural lands, and a tendency for the arable to be extended on to the thinner upland soils. Both developments would have required a considerable increase in the provision of manure, and in a landscape such as this the only animal able to provide it was the sheep which could exist for long periods on unwatered uplands. The increase in numbers of sheep should, then, be seen not as reflecting a decline in the importance of cattle but as the response of the economic system to the stimulus of increased population. Large flocks of sheep imposed on the system a newly available surplus – wool – which may well have affected other areas of the socio-economic system.

Towards the end of the occupation of Danebury in the second century BC there are vague hints of possible stress in the animal population. Most noticeable is that sheep have risen in proportion and more of them are showing periodontal disease (disease of the mouth). Another factor is the significant decline in the percentage of pig, possibly reflecting the over-use and demise of woodland pannage.

This chapter has concentrated almost entirely on the food staples which leave their mark on the archaeological record, but this should not be allowed to obscure the vast range of other foods and relishes that would have been collected and eaten – fish, birds' eggs, berries, fruits, roots, fungi and honey. The environment was rich with an inexhaustible supply of these commodities and the community was no doubt expert in seeking them out. There would also have been more exotic delicacies like kittiwake brought up from the coast, perhaps with a load of salt. These are mere hints of the extremely rich and varied fare that would have enlivened the predominantly cereal diet of the inhabitants.

8

Craft, exchange and luxury

Most of the everyday needs of the society at Danebury were met by local craft production on or close to the site, using readily available raw materials such as clay, chalk, wood, bone, antler, leather, sinew, wool, straw and reeds. In most peasant societies the skills needed to manipulate these substances were always available in the family group and there is no need to suppose a high degree of craft specialization, although it is normal for productive tasks to be divided between age and sex groups. In one Berber community in north-western Tunisia, for example, the men and young boys dig the potting clay and bring it to the homestead. The old women usually make the basic pottery forms while the younger women add decoration and see to the firing. Sadly, details of this kind are seldom likely to be recognizable in the archaeological record.

Pottery

The Danebury community used a great deal of pottery: nearly 160,000 sherds were found! Its study is of great importance in providing a chronology for the site but it is also extremely informative from the point of view of craft and trade.

In the early period (500–400 BC) two basic pottery forms were in use: fairly shallow open bowls, usually made in fine sandy fabrics; and larger jars, used for storage and cooking, made in much coarser gritty wares (**70**). The grits were a deliberately added tempering of crushed flint and crushed shell, mixed in to bulk out the clay of the heavier vessels to make it stronger and less susceptible to cracking during firing. The bowls were of two types: simple undecorated vessels made from quite coarse sandy clays; and also extremely finely made bowls decorated with cordons on the shoulders and scratched decoration, with the outside of the body coated with bright red burnished haematite (see **70**). The differences between the two types are so striking that there can be little doubt that the 'scratched cordoned bowls' (SCBs) were expertly made as a high value product, while the remaining vessels could easily have been manufactured in the fort or close by, by the local community.

At this time all pottery was made by hand, usually by building up the form with coils of clay, and sealing the joints by pulling the coils together with the fingers. The coarse wares were seldom decorated, except for finger pushing on the shoulder or rim top, giving a pie-crust effect, but the surfaces were often wiped over with a handful of grass or, in the case of the bowls, with leather or a fine fabric, to smooth the clay and give a shiny appearance. After being allowed to dry naturally for a while the pots would be stacked in a heap, covered with wood chippings and brushwood and domed over with turves, leaving a few air vents around the sides. When complete the clamp would be fired and left for a day or two to burn itself out. The dome could then be pulled away and the fired pots extricated from the ashes. The method sounds rather primitive but experiments have shown it to be extremely simple to operate, usually producing excellent results. Archaeologically it leaves no distinctive traces and we are therefore unlikely ever to be sure where pottery was being manufactured. The very simplicity of the method, however, would allow it to have been carried out close to the home in any general working area.

The fine, scratched cordoned bowls required far more care and skill in their production. In

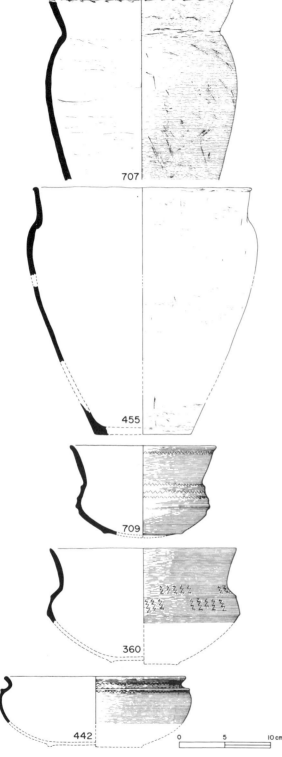

the first place brickearth, a very fine sandy clay, was selected to allow a thin fabric, sometimes only 4mm (⅛in) thick, to be produced. The bowls, with their sharp angles, may have been made partly by the slab method which involved the components being beaten into shape (possibly in leather moulds) and then pieced together. When the basic form was complete the cordons were raised with a bone modelling tool, which may then have been used to burnish the surface finely. The vessel was next dipped into a red slip, made of a watered down clay base mixed with crushed haematite or another oxide of iron, and then left to dry. Further burnishing was needed to seal the slip before, finally, a simple geometric decoration was scratched into the surface using a sharp metal point. The firing stage was probably the most difficult because the vessels had to be stacked in such a way that they did not distort each other and the clamp had to be so arranged that an adequate supply of air was allowed at all times to ensure that the pots were fired in an oxidizing atmosphere to give the characteristic red colour.

The scratched cordoned bowls, dating as they do to the sixth century BC, represent a highly sophisticated level of potting which can fairly be regarded as the work of specialists. Petrological analysis of the fabrics shows that the clay most frequently used was a brickearth of a variety occurring near Salisbury in the very centre of the distribution range of the type. This is another indication that we are dealing with specialists (not necessarily full time) who were supplying a region. But it would be wrong to think in terms of commercial supply since the vessels may well have been distributed as prestige goods through social mechanisms such as gift exchange. If this was so the distribution of the bowls would reflect the extent of a territory linked by social ties (**71**).

By the middle period the fine scratched cordoned bowls had ceased to be made and other changes are observable in the pottery assemblage. The fabrics, for example, were becoming more sandy as grit and shell fillers became less popular. In addition the vessels were now more often well-smoothed and burnished before firing; the clamps in which they were made seem to have been more carefully controlled to give evenly fired black surfaces to the vessels. In short the domestic, as opposed to specialist, ceramic techniques were improving.

70 *Pottery of the early period c.550–450 BC. Nos. 709, 360 and 442 are 'haematite' coated.*

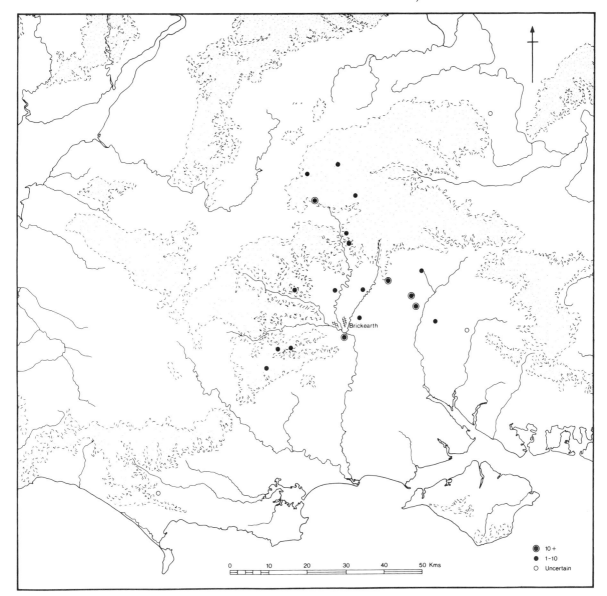

Brickearth

⦿	10 +
●	1-10
○	Uncertain

0   10   20   30   40   50 Kms

71 *The distribution of the scratched cordoned bowls. The brickearth deposit may have been the source of the clay from which they were made.*

The late period, starting *c.* 350 BC, saw further improvements and an even greater degree of standardization. To begin with sandy fabrics predominated but gradually they were replaced with fine flint-grit tempered wares. The vessel forms were now limited to a range of jars with inturned mouths, large jars with outcurved rims, open pans and straight-sided saucepan pots. There seems to have been little further

change in form throughout the late period.

The normal finish for all late vessels was a smooth burnished surface fired black. Many were decorated and as time progressed so the percentage of decorated wares increased (**72**). The method of decoration differed from that of the early period. The vessels were now ornamented, when leather-hard, with a bone point with which the potter gently incised geometric patterns of lines and dots in horizontal zones. This 'shallow tooled' decoration became very popular in southern Britain by the second century BC, with each region displaying favoured motifs.

The vast bulk of the shallow tooled decorated

89

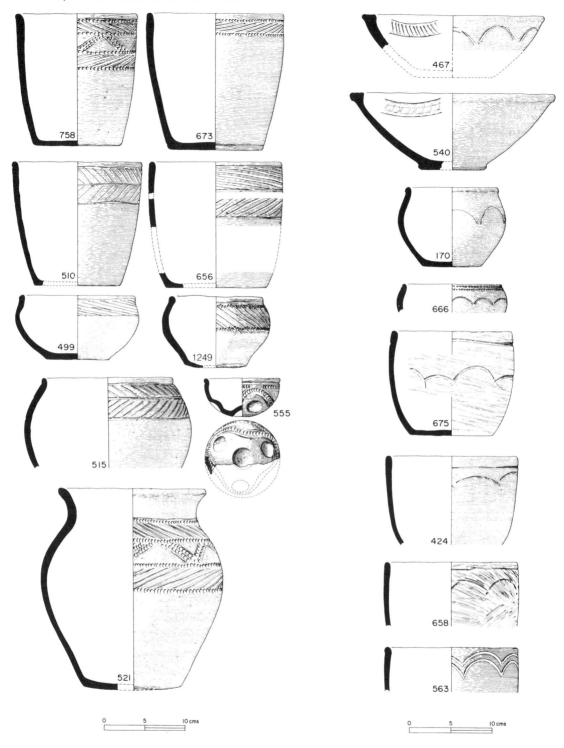

72 *Decorated pottery of the late period c.350–100 BC made from 'local' flint-tempered clay.*

73 *Decorated pottery of the late period c.350–100 BC made from glauconitic clay from Wiltshire.*

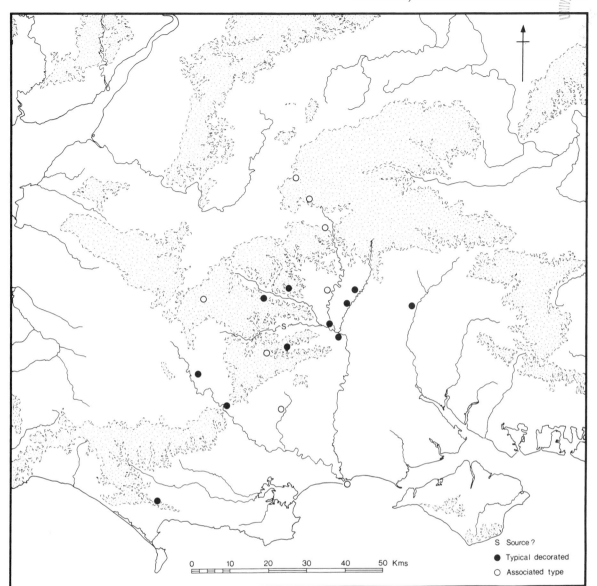

74 *The distribution of Late Wiltshire glauconitic wares.*

ware at Danebury belongs to a style-zone stretching from the coast in the south to the Kennet Valley in the north and from the river Arun in Sussex to the Bourne Valley just west of Danebury. Danebury is on the western edge of this distribution and, as might be expected, decorative styles from the adjacent Wiltshire region are also found (**73**). The Wiltshire potters favoured the pendant arc motif, often with indentations at the intersections, while the Hampshire potters were particularly fond of

horizontal zones filled with diagonal hatching and sometimes delineated with borders of dots. One group of the Wiltshire decorated pots was made in a sandy fabric containing minerals found in the valley of the river Nadder, 35km (22 miles) west of Danebury. Since it is highly unlikely that raw clay would have been carried this far to Danebury it is best to regard the pots as imports, brought to Danebury, no doubt, more for their contents than their intrinsic value (see **73**).

The pottery has been dealt with at some length because it does provide a range of useful insights into the workings of the community;

but in their enthusiasm archaeologists often forget that pottery was actually used by the people to store, transport, prepare and serve food. The jars, for example, were adequate for heating liquids over the fire but would more often have been used as convenient storage containers for dry foods like cereals or for milk or water. Jars with flared rims were well designed to take a skin cover which could be tied in place around the neck. The smaller bowls of the early period and the saucepan pots of the later were probably used to serve food. The open pans could also have functioned in this way but another possibility is that they were skimming pans in which cream was allowed to form as a preliminary to cheese making.

Other raw materials

Pottery vessels will have served a range of domestic functions but more durable containers could be made, quite easily, from wood. No trace of these survives at Danebury but in the waterlogged conditions prevailing at the Iron Age sites of Glastonbury and Meare (Somerset), an impressive collection has come to light. Some of the tub-shaped vessels are very much like the saucepan pots and may indeed have provided the inspiration for the saucepan-pot form. Other small domestic containers were no doubt made from bark and leather and it has been suggested that the favoured decorative motif, incorporating diagonal lines between rows of dots, could be a copy in pottery of stitching patterns on leather containers.

Other organic materials vital to domestic life, but leaving little or no evidence on a site like Danebury, include basketry and matting. Suitable raw materials were readily available. Small knives, of which there are many, would have been the only manufacturing tool needed. Baskets, mats, wicker covers and screens and a host of other items of the same kind no doubt abounded in the settlement. Wickerwork had other uses, for example in making fish traps, but of these and of fishing nets that were probably used in the fast flowing waters of the river Test we know nothing.

Two of the most important by-products of the flocks and herds were leather and wool, both of which were treated on the site. We know comparatively little of leather dressing techniques in the Iron Age but the processes can be conjectured. Once the skin was removed it would be pegged out on the ground and the under surface scraped with iron knives, over a period of several weeks, to remove the remaining fat and soft tissue. Then salt or wood ash would be rubbed into the surface as a preservative. There is no direct evidence that tanning was carried out but it was comparatively easy to do, as the Roman historian Pliny reminds us, using the galls caused by wasps on oak leaves as a source of tannin.

Hides had many uses, for making clothing, containers, thongs, harness and saddles, and could be very easily worked with sharp iron knives and iron awls for making holes before sewing. A constant supply of leather would have been needed to meet the demands of the community and it remains a possibility that a surplus may have been accumulated for exchange, though there is little in the animal bone assemblage to suggest an economy geared to leather production.

Textiles

Wool was produced in quantity and constitutes what can fairly be called an industry, for the output must have exceeded local consumption. The hairy sheep of the Iron Age could be plucked with ease in the moulting season, a task which may have been aided with long-handled combs made of bone and antler (75). These so-called 'weaving combs' were general purpose tools useful in the various stages of the textile manufacturing process. Raw wool would be cleaned, sorted for colour and carded before hand spinning on a simple wooden spindle weighted with a spindle whorl of stone or baked clay. Once the skeins of thread had been produced they could, if necessary, be dyed with a wide range of vegetable dyes.

Weaving was carried out on a vertical warp-weighted loom, the vertical threads (warp) being held taut by heavy weights of chalk or clay to which the warp threads were tied in bundles. The weaving of the weft would begin at the top, using a threader of bone attached to some kind of shuttle, and to push the weft tightly into place it is likely that a wooden 'sword' was used as a beater. For finer cloths or braids the weaving combs would have been useful.

Archaeological evidence for textile manufacture is extensive at Danebury, as it is at many Iron Age sites in central southern Britain. Spindle whorls, loom weights, weaving combs

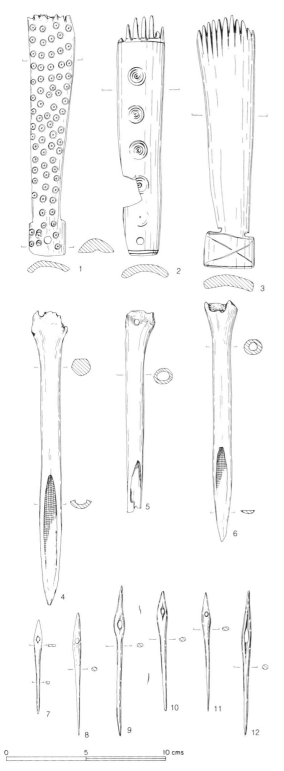

and threaders are found on most sites but not always in equal quantities. Danebury, for example, produced a far greater number of loom weights in relation to spindle whorls than is usual at the neighbouring farmstead sites, where spindle whorls were dominant. While these differences and similarities may be completely fortuitous, they could be interpreted as showing that proportionately more weaving was carried out in the hillforts and, if so, it could be suggested that skeins spun at the farmsteads were being taken to the fort, possibly as tribute, there to be woven into cloth. The possibility is intriguing and carries with it implications for the social position of the hillfort dwellers (see below pp. 108–10).

What was then done with this cloth is a matter of debate but woollen garments for the occupants would have been the first call. Roman writers describing the British Queen Boudica in the first century AD mention her multicoloured clothing – a reference which gives a fleeting impression of brightly coloured tartan. But if the suggestion of a significant overproduction is correct, what form did the surplus take? Sadly we will never know but in some societies, like the North West Coast Indians of Canada, surplus was converted into blankets which could be distributed in complex forms of gift exchange or actually destroyed in potlatch ceremonies designed to establish the status of competing individuals. In other words surplus, in this society, was converted into a modular form – the blanket – which could be used in social and economic transactions. Whether or not the wool of the Danebury sheep was transformed in this way is impossible to say but the use of the wool, in some kind of manufactured form, for transactions between the fort and other communities seems highly likely.

Woodworking

One of the basic raw materials of enormous value to the community was wood. Wood has already been considered in its structural guise, for building houses, grain stores and defences, but the range of everyday uses to which it would have been put is endless. Of great importance to the community were ards and wheeled vehicles. While an ard could be made by any intelligent being, the carpenter building a cart or war chariot was very probably a highly skilled specialist. The balance of the vehicle,

75 *Bone weaving equipment: 1–3 'weaving combs'; 4–6 threaders; 7–12 needles.*

the arrangement of the axles and base and the steering mechanism was complex enough but the construction of spoked wheels needed a craftsman of a high order. By this time the techniques of shrinking-on an iron tyre were being widely practised. Evidence of carts at Danebury is limited to a pair of linchpins, fragments of iron tyres and two pairs of hub bindings. Linchpins were slotted through the axle ends to prevent the wheels from working loose and falling off. Quite often they were elaborately decorated with cast bronze heads but the Danebury examples were relatively plain as would befit a work-a-day cart rather than a flashy war chariot. An elaborate decorated example made in iron and bronze was found at Bury Hill (**77**).

Metalworking

Three raw materials of very considerable importance to the community had to be imported from outside the immediate territory of the fort – iron, bronze and stone. Little is known about the systems involved in extracting and distributing iron during the British Iron Age because little of the necessary analytical work has yet been undertaken, but iron was probably being extracted from a variety of sources and transported from the smelting sites, in ingot form, to the settlements where the forging was carried out. The nearest large sources of iron ore to Danebury lay in north Wiltshire and the Weald, or further afield in the Forest of Dean, but smaller, more localized sources can be found closer at hand in the Tertiary rocks of the Hampshire basin as, for example, at Hengistbury Head on the Dorset coast. The first analyses available hint that the Weald was possibly the prime source for Danebury but more work is required before we can be sure.

The extraction of iron involved a comparatively simple technology requiring the ore to be roasted first and then heated in a reducing atmosphere to above 700°C (1292°F). At this temperature the oxide was reduced to the metal, and the waste products melted and flowed into the furnace base leaving a bun-sized spongy mass of iron known as a bloom. The blooms had then to be reheated and hammered to drive out impurities in the form of hammer scale. A number of blooms were probably forged together to make an ingot of manageable size. By the second century BC the

76 *Hoard of scrap iron during excavation.*

ingots had become standardized into shapes of recognizable form known as 'currency bars' – a term deriving from a remark of Julius Caesar's that the Britons traded with bars of iron as well as with coins. The most common shape for these bars in Britain was in the form of long flat strips with pinched up 'handles' vaguely similar in size and shape to swords. A hoard of 21 of these sword-shaped currency bars was found in building CS22, bundled up and packed tightly into a shallow pit dug into the floor. This amount of metal would probably have had a quite considerable value.

The average bar weighed about 450g (16 oz), large enough to make several small tools. A number of fragmentary bars were found showing that the complete ingots were probably cut up, on site, into lengths convenient for forging into tools. That forging was carried out on a large scale is amply demonstrated by a scatter of forging slag found in rubbish deposits throughout the fort. There are also pieces of furnace base and fragments of tuyères, the baked clay nozzles of bellows. No site within the fort has yet been identified as a smithy but the concentration of ironworking debris in the southern zone close to the rampart is an indication that this sheltered position may have been favoured.

Bronze is found in very much smaller quantities probably because it was carefully collected for reuse. The presence of various fragments of bronze-working crucibles scattered about the site shows that specialists were at work melting down scrap for recasting. There were two

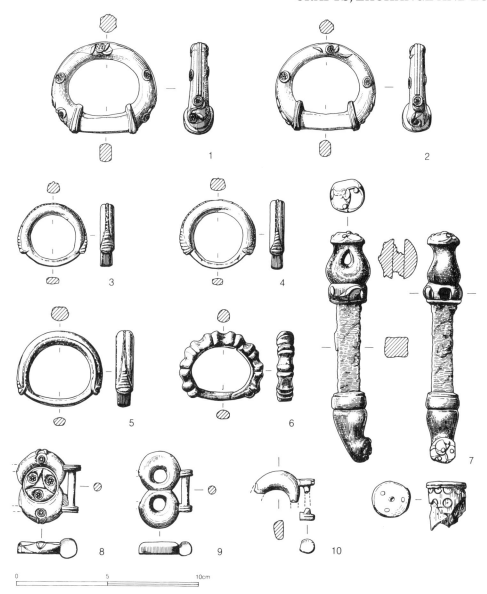

77 *Horse gear from Bury Hill. Strap junctions, terrets and a linchpin.*

principal types of bronze-working practised at this time: casting and sheet bronze work. Sheet bronze was widely used for making bowls, cauldrons, scabbards, scabbard bindings and decorative shield coverings. Little can be said of the comparatively sparse Danebury collection except that bronze vessels and scabbard bindings are well represented, but analysis has shown that the bronze smiths favoured a special alloy with an unusually high cobalt and nickel content, possibly coming from the south-

west of England. This could mean either that the objects themselves were made in the south-west and exported, or alternatively, the bronze smiths were careful to use a preferred alloy for all sheet bronze products.

The alloy used for the cast bronze items was more varied and may, indeed, be recycled scrap. Objects were cast by the *cire perdu* (lost wax) process. This involved making a beeswax model of the object and carefully coating it in clay, leaving channels between the wax and the outside. When the clay was dry it was heated so that the wax melted and could be poured off: heating was then increased to bake the mould hard. The actual casting process simply involved pouring the molten bronze into the mould to fill the space occupied by the wax. The mould could then be broken open and the casting cleaned and finely tooled to remove blemishes and, occasionally, to add decorative detail by chasing with a fine chisel or scriber. These were the processes by which the fine decorative harness fittings found in house CS7/8 as well as those from Bury Hill were made (see **77**).

Although a number of crucible fragments were found at Danebury no mould fragment has yet come to light, but at Gussage All Saints, an Iron Age farmstead in Dorset, a considerable quantity of broken moulds was found discarded in a pit together with other bronze-working debris. An analysis of the discards suggests that this one deposit resulted from the manufacture of 50 sets of horse gear! Clearly a specialist was at work here making sufficient gear to serve a very large area.

Stone

While supplies of iron and bronze were manipulated by specialists at various stages between the extraction of the raw material and the final production of the finished item, stone was a rather more accessible commodity requiring comparatively little skilled preparation. Stone was used for a variety of purposes, but principally to make quernstones, weights and whetstones. The most prolific were the quernstones, used for grinding corn. No suitable stone was to be found in the immediate vicinity but usable greensand was available in the region of Shaftesbury, Westbury and the Vale of Wardour between 30 and 50km (20 and 30 miles) away, sources which produced 78 per cent of all the stone found on the site. Other querns were made from Tertiary sandstone, probably from the Hampshire basin, and from gritstones likely to have come from the Mendips up to 80km (50 miles) to the west, but the quantity of the latter was small (less than 3 per cent). Since quernstones were constantly wearing out regular supplies had to be maintained: no community with a cereal-based diet could afford to be without.

The stone weights present a rather more varied range of rock types. Of the 68 examples found, 38 were of greensand, ten of Tertiary sandstone, two of carboniferous limestone and the others of six other rock types mainly from

78 *Stone weight. The shank of a broken iron ring projects from the top (half size).*

the west of England but including a limestone from Bembridge in the Isle of Wight. These stone weights raise extremely interesting questions. They are all carefully finished and many of them still retain iron rings set in a hole in the top for ease of suspension (**78**). The simplest explanation of their function is that they formed part of a system of accurate measurement for weighing out commodities like corn or wool, but at first sight the apparent range of weights represented poses problems: they vary from just over 600g (21oz) to more than 4300g (152oz) with no obvious clustering of particular weights, and there were too few for statistical treatment to be applied to isolate standards from the weights themselves. If the weights are for measurement in some kind of exchange system then the wide range of stone present might in some way reflect the areas with which exchange was being undertaken.

The whetstones, essentially unworked pebbles suitable for sharpening metal implements, reflect a similarly wide range of source location. The 74 examples were made from 18 different kinds of stone, including igneous rocks from the south-west, and slates, mudstones and sandstones from the Devonian and carboniferous rocks of Devon and Somerset. They could all have been brought to the site as low value items of exchange in the complex patterns of social and economic intercourse in operation at the time.

Salt

One necessity which no community which depended on a predominantly cereal-based diet could afford to neglect was salt. Salt was an essential additive to the human diet; it was also useful in preserving meat and in the treatment of skins. There were two principal sources: salt-rich springs like those at Droitwich, and sea water. In both cases the salt cake produced was packed into clay containers for ease of transport. Fragments of these clay containers, known as briquetage, survive in rubbish layers and can be readily identified.

The salt imported into Danebury came from the coast of Dorset and Hampshire, where evidence of the industry has been found at a number of sites. The first stage in the extraction process would have been the collection of sea water in pans on the shore where the heat of the summer sun would concentrate it. The salt-rich liquor could then be evaporated artificially in clay trays over fires and the salt cake produced packed in briquetage containers. Some of these containers were like small hemispherical jars but others were in the form of open-topped cylinders which had been cut vertically into two halves. This curious arrangement may have been to allow the container of salt (the two halves bound together in some way), to be divided into two equal measures. If the containers were of uniform size then the half measures would have had a recognizable value. Unfortunately the briquetage fragments so far available are too small to allow sizes to be estimated and without this it is impossible to test the question of standardization.

Shale

Another commodity imported from the south coast was Kimmeridge shale which outcropped on the Dorset coast in a comparatively limited area where, incidentally, there is also ample evidence of contemporary salt-working activity. Kimmeridge shale, in its freshly quarried state, is a black oily shale which can be easily cut and highly polished. In the Iron Age, as indeed in the Roman period, it was widely used to make armlets (or anklets), and less frequently, rings and beads. Magical properties may have been ascribed to it as they were to jet.

The shale was dug out of the cliff face and worked in the many settlements clustering on the Isle of Purbeck, either into the finished items or into annular roughouts requiring further treatment. In both forms it was exported widely, being found in Iron Age settlements as far apart as Kent and Cornwall. A number of armlet fragments, four beads and at least two roughouts have been found at Danebury, but that so little has been recovered from such a comparatively large excavation is some indication of the rarity of the material.

Other ornaments are even rarer. Several coloured glass beads were recovered together with three beads of amber and one small fragment of pink coral (**79**). No doubt items of this kind had a considerable value and would move through the social system as gifts, or with wives, until they were lost, or in one case at Danebury, buried on the neck of a female.

The movement of goods

Little has yet been said of the way in which these items and materials were moved about society at large, nor have we discussed the relationship between developed hillforts like Danebury and other settlements. This whole subject is fraught with difficulties. The first point to emphasize is that trade, as we know it, was probably not practised in pre-Roman Britain, rather commodities were exchanged in a variety of ways dictated by the social system. There would be gift exchange between equals, the passing of high-value goods from a patron to a client in recognition of status differences and in return for a different range of goods and services, bride price and dowries, tribute and, of course, the spoils of warfare. Even skilled craftsmen would have been constrained within the social structure by the power of their patrons. A bronze smith, for example, might have produced sets of horse gear for his patron, which were then distributed as gifts to others, or his services might have been made available to another man of rank in return for an equivalent level of service. An economic system which works in this way, articulated by the social system, is referred to as an embedded economy. In such a system it is impossible to separate the social structure from the economic. A detailed discussion about the nature of society will follow in the next chapter, here the more general mechanics which may have been in operation will be outlined.

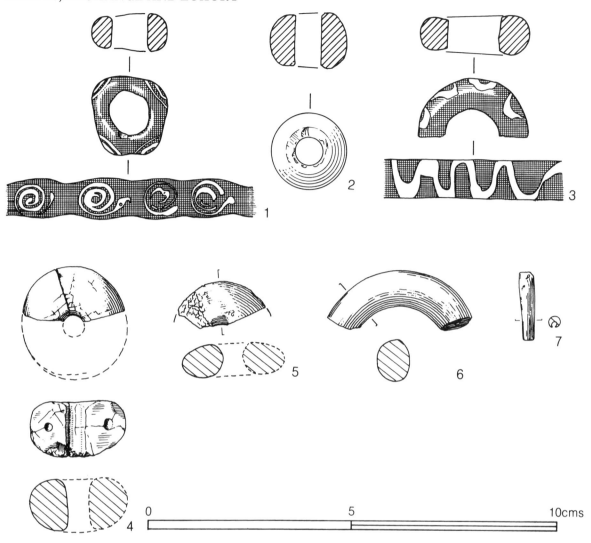

79 *Ornaments: 1–3 beads of glass; 4–6 beads of amber; 7 bead of coral.*

A developed hillfort like Danebury was very different from the early hillforts of Wessex and also from the contemporary farmsteads which cluster so thickly on the ground. Its social status was different and so was its economic position in the landscape. One aspect of these differences, which can be roughly quantified, is pit storage capacity. The figures available show that not only was the fort of larger area than the average farmstead but it was also more densely packed with pits. As already noted, a rough comparison suggests that developed hill-forts like Danebury had something like twenty times the storage pit capacity of a typical farm.

If the 'granary' storage capacity is added then the figure is greatly increased. Even on a very conservative estimate, allowing that not all the pits and granaries were for grain storage, the total grain storage capacity of such a fort was well in excess of the productive capacity of the land that could have been farmed directly from it. Moreover the stored grain could have supported a very much larger population than is likely to have been resident in the fort.

The implication of all this is that the fort had the capacity for storing the surplus grain product of a considerable territory. This is supported by the analysis of the weed seeds present in the grain sample, which shows that crops were being brought to the fort from the damp lands of the river valleys and the clay-capped hills to

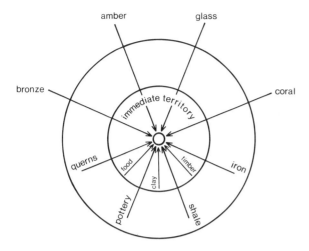

80 *The sources of the raw materials used at Danebury (in the centre) coming from the immediate territory (inner ring), neighbouring territories (outer ring) and from distant locations.*

the north, all some distance away. Why society should have contributed part of its surplus to the fort will be considered later (pp. 108–12), but for whatever reason it would have led to some form of centralized distribution mechanism coming into force – a community sending a tithe of its produce to the fort would have had something in return. If, for example, it was the patronage of a lord this may well have taken with it the passing of some other commodity, under the lord's control, down the system to the farm-based community.

Redistribution mechanisms of this kind can be seen in many earlier societies. In the valleys of the Tigris and Euphrates the Sumerians contributed to the temple granaries, while in Crete Minoan surplus was deposited in the store rooms of the palaces. But the result would have been much the same: the authority of the central location, whether religious or secular, drew in surplus and consolidated it. This enabled other raw materials to be acquired from outside the territory and provided the context for them to be manufactured into a variety of goods which then entered the system and flowed in the reverse direction. A practical example of this might entail a peasant farmer's

sending a tithe of his crop to an overlord and in return receiving not only patronage and protection but also presents of manufactured goods or rare raw materials. These transactions are embedded in the social system.

Whether or not such a simple redistribution model works for the kind of Iron Age society under discussion is not easy to determine. All that can be done is to compare the data from Danebury with the model to see how good is the fit (**80**).

To begin with there is ample evidence to suggest that two basic commodities, grain and wool, were probably produced in surplus and may well have been concentrated in the hillfort. Both commodities could have been used in external transactions. Fleeces or woollen garments given to the local chieftain commanding the main routes south through the Hampshire basin, may well have elicited gifts of salt or Kimmeridge shale in return, while grain, given to western neighbours, might have facilitated the flow of quernstones or metals. If the gift exchange, involving these commodities, was at the social level represented by the developed hillforts, then the gifts flowing in would concentrate here before being divided up and passed on to clients. Another aspect of the model would see a part of the surplus supporting specialists who offered services – some might be blacksmiths converting currency bars into useful tools, while others might be the priests and wise men needed to provide the broader community with its legal and religious focus.

If this is really what was happening at Danebury it would explain the enhanced storage capacity, the temples, the metalworking activity, the emphasis on weaving, the iron ingots and salt containers, and the weight standards. Individually these classes of evidence could be explained away and it could be argued that many of the same activities are also to be found on contemporary farmsteads. This is so, but all the evidence taken together and the sheer intensity of activity at Danebury in the late period compared to what was going on in the countryside around, provides very strong circumstantial evidence to suggest that developed hillforts like Danebury performed an important redistributive function in articulating the exchange systems in society.

9

The social order

By its very nature archaeological evidence enables us to understand the structural history of a site and to analyse the economic systems at work in some detail, but approaching the people themselves and the organization of their society is a far more difficult problem. This is particularly true of the Iron Age communities of southern Britain for whom burial evidence is very sparse, but piecing together the scraps that survive enables us to begin to glimpse something of the very complex world of ritual and belief that pervaded Iron Age society.

Religion

The gods were everywhere. It is probably no exaggeration to say that every act in a man's life was circumscribed by some kind of ritual or taboo. The Celtic year for example was composed of twelve lunar months each divided into a light and a dark half which had considerable influence on a man's actions. On the famous calendar found at Coligny in France, each month was annotated to say whether it was 'good' or 'not good', that is auspicious or otherwise. Information of this kind would have been essential to a war leader deciding when to lead an expedition or to a farmer wanting to know when to begin to sow his fields. The influence of 'propitious time' is also clearly brought out by the Roman writer Pliny in describing the Druidic ritual involved in cutting mistletoe:

> They choose groves of oak for the sake of the trees alone and they never perform any sacred rite unless they have a branch of it. They think that everything that grows on it has been sent from heaven and by the God himself. Mistletoe, however, is very rarely found on the oak and when it is it is gathered with great ceremony, if possible on the sixth

day of the moon . . . They choose this day because, although the moon has not yet reached half size, it has already got considerable influence.

Thus for every action there was an appropriate time and only a rash man would ignore the fact.

The gods, too, had to be propitiated. A major work like building a rampart would, no doubt, have been accompanied by a complex of rituals involving sacrifices and foundation burials. Some hint of this was found at Danebury on the north side of the fort at the time when the rampart was reconstructed. In the bottom of the freshly dug quarry hollow a large shallow pit was dug and three bodies were laid out in it before it was carefully refilled with chalk rubble (**81**). The unusual nature of the deposit and its position in relation to the rampart sequence strongly suggest some kind of propitiatory rite.

Ritual animal burials in pits

On a more domestic scale, the digging of a grain storage pit for seed grain was heavily circumscribed by ritual behaviour. After all, the domain of the gods of the underworld was being penetrated and society was putting its trust in the gods to preserve the fertility of the crop stored in the ground. It was a risky thing to do unless the proper rituals had been upheld. The crucial time would have come at the end of the storage period when the pit was emptied and the seed was sown. At such a time the gods had to be placated with a propitiatory offering if fertility was to be ensured. Not surprisingly there is ample evidence that something of the sort was carried out on a large scale at Danebury.

The evidence of ritual behaviour comes in the

81 *Three male corpses buried in a single pit in the bottom of the quarry hollow on the north side of the fort. Possibly a ritual foundation burial.*

form of special deposits on pit bottoms or low down in pit fills. These include groups of pots, iron implements, layers of burnt grain and animal burials. While each individual case could be explained away in non-ritual terms the sheer number of these depositions and the recurring patterns to be found strongly suggest that they represent the archaeological evidence for a complex pattern of behaviour.

The special animal deposits provide the most extensive body of information (**82–83**). They fall into three broad categories: articulated skeletons; complete or nearly complete skulls and mandibles (always horse); and articulated limbs. The animals represented were sheep, cattle, pigs, horses and dogs, with a single example of a cat and a skull and a skeleton of a goat. Complete animal burials occurred in 5 per cent of the Danebury pits, skulls and horse mandibles in 12 per cent and articulated limbs in 3 per cent.

Many of the articulated skeletons represent complete carcasses and the absence of butchery marks on the bones suggests that the beasts were not even skinned before burial. There were, however, some cases in which the animals were partly dismembered. In pit 321, for example, a horse was buried with a dog (see **82**). The horse was largely intact but one front and one back leg were slightly displaced and the head had been removed and placed behind the body next to the dog. While this might have resulted from the burial of a partially decomposed carcass, it may be that the removal of the legs and head formed part of the ritual – a view to some extent supported by the fact that horse heads and horse legs were not infrequently found buried separately.

101

82 *Ritual burial of a partially dismembered horse and a dog.*

Birds also featured in the special burials. The majority were ravens, and since this in no way reflects the natural bird population of southern Britain, it could only have happened if ravens had been specially selected. Only 12 per cent of the pits produced bird bones but more than a third of these were found in pits which also contained special animal burials. Statistical tests show that these associations are unlikely to have happened by chance.

These rather random observations are sufficient to indicate that something deliberate was influencing the treatment and burial of animals at Danebury and similar evidence is available from other Iron Age sites, including Bury Hill and Suddern Farm, to show that Danebury was by no means unique. The actions and beliefs leading to the selection and treatment

of the animal victims before deposition were evidently complex and only by observing even larger samples will the range of behaviour begin to sort itself into patterns. But even at this early stage a distinction is discernible between the offerings of the principal food animals – sheep, cattle and pig – and the burial of more exotic creatures – the dog, horse and raven – which in Celtic mythology have more complex connotations. For example the dog is often found associated with Celtic deities in mythology and iconography; the Celtic goddess Epona ('divine horse') is usually depicted seated on a horse (often, incidentally, with a dog by her side); while the raven-god is a recurring theme in magico-religious literature of Gaul and Ireland.

While the special animal burials are the most numerous of the depositions in pits, the layers of grain, groups of pots and occasional iron tools, could all reflect the desire to dedicate part

83 *Horse skull placed on the bottom of a pit.*

of society's wealth to the gods in propitiatory acts, especially if the pots had contained food or drink. Taken all together, about a third of the pits contain evidence of this kind, and this raises the question of the remaining two thirds – were they abandoned without a propitiatory offering being made or did they, too, once contain offerings of which no archaeological trace remains? Bales of wool, cheeses, or a libation of milk, mead or blood would leave no obvious signs.

Human burials

Another kind of deposit found in the pits, which presumably also has a ritual significance, is the deposition of human remains represented by whole or fragmentary skeletons (**84–88**). In total some 300 different depositions of human bones were discovered, most of them in pits. The burials display a very varied range of ritual behaviour but basically they can be divided into two principal categories: the inhumation of whole bodies soon after death but before the flesh had decayed sufficiently to allow the body to fall apart; and the deposition of skeletal remains some time after the connective tissue had begun to rot.

The complete inhumations were represented by 38 bodies ranging in age from neonatal to about 45, but the sample does not appear to reflect a normal stable population structure. There is, for example, a preponderance of adult males (leaving aside the neonatal interments, 39 per cent are males aged 14–35) and the number of fertile females and newly-born infants is less than would be expected. While this could be a mere accident of survival, it is safer to assume that the sample fairly reflects the total, in which case bodies buried in this way were selected from among those who died.

Within the category of complete inhumations two slightly different burial rituals can be distinguished: the burial of individuals, and burial in groups of two, three or more. The orientation of the bodies and details of the subsequent filling above the skeletons further support the view that two distinct rituals are involved but other aspects are similar – for example the bodies are usually in a flexed or crouched position and are never provided with grave goods.

The second major type of burial ritual involves the deposition of part of a human body and since (with one exception to be described later) no sign of deliberate dismemberment has been noted, it is likely that what was being

103

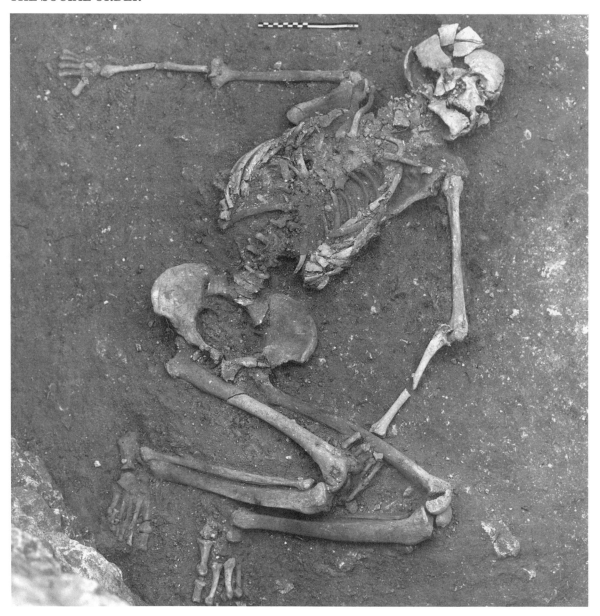

84 *Human body thrown into a pit.*

buried were the disintegrated remnants of rotted corpses. These partial bodies can be divided into several categories of deposition: individual incomplete skeletons; groups of incomplete skeletons; skulls and frontal bones; pelvic girdles; and individual bones and bone fragments. A typical incomplete individual was the female aged 20–30 whose remains were found in pit 266 on top of a layer of ash and charcoal. Her spinal column and sacrum had been removed

from the pelvis and laid around her feet and lower legs but her right fibula, right scapula, left clavicle, both arms and head were missing. The absence of heads and arms is a recurring feature in a number of cases while in another group, usually children, it is the lower limbs and pelvic girdles that are missing. There is sufficient patterning in this group to suggest that parts of the body were deliberately being removed before the remnants were placed in pits.

Two pits, pits 923 and 1078, contained collections of partially dismembered bodies, ten and

85 *Human body tightly folded and placed against the overhanging side of a pit.*

11 respectively, dumped together in a heap. Men, women and children are represented but the assemblage in pit 1078 is dominated by children over eight and adult males in the older age bracket. There is no evidence of butchery or violent dismemberment and the manner of deposition suggests that the bodies were thrown into their respective pits after the flesh had decayed. That some were more complete than others might indicate that the corpses had rotted for different lengths of time before final deposition. Both pits also contained special animal burials.

Isolated human skulls complete or largely complete were found in 15 pits (**87**). Of those identifiable, seven belong to young males between the ages of 17 and 35, four to juveniles and three to females. This is sufficient evidence

to suggest that male heads were being afforded special treatment and it may be that this is archaeological evidence of the Celtic head-hunting ritual described below (pp. 106–7). That the majority of the skulls were found in pits of the latest phase (cp 7) may indicate that the ritual gained in popularity with time. Several of them had suffered from severe head wounds immediately before death.

Pelvic girdles, either whole or fragmentary, were also selected for isolated burial. The example found in pit 1020 is unusual in that it is the only fragment of a human body to show positive signs of butchery (**89**). The pelvis was of a young man aged between 18 and 25. It seems that the legs were probably removed first by hacking through the upper ends of each femur shaft with a combination of longitudinal and horizontal chopping strokes. The pelvis was then freed from the torso by cutting through the soft tissues of the lower trunk and then chopping the spine in the vicinity of the first sacral vertebra. It took several blows to sever all the back muscles. This gruesome task seems to have been carried out with a narrow bladed weapon like a sword rather than a knife or an axe. When freed from the rest of the body the pelvis was placed on the bottom of a bath-shaped pit together with the skull of a pig, another fragment of human bone, and some fragments of quernstone before the deposit was sealed with a layer of puddled chalk.

Finally, isolated human bones were found in 211 contexts. This was not a random scatter, as would be expected if old burials had been disturbed, but a sample deliberately biased towards certain bones. The femur occurs more often than any other bone and the long bones of the right side of the body are more common than those of the left. These biases are true for all periods and must mean that certain parts of corpses were being removed, presumably for ritual purposes.

Standing back from the rather distasteful details rehearsed above, something of the general picture begins to come into focus. It is now reasonably certain that regular inhumation in cemeteries was not practised by the Iron Age communities of southern Britain but instead the rites of passage for the dead were infinitely more complex. The complete inhumations (leaving aside the possible foundation burial of three males in the northern quarry hollow) may be the result of the disposal of the

86 (Above) *Tumbled human remains in a charnel pit.*

bodies of those considered unclean or inhuman – people robbed of normal burial and disposed of with the rubbish, in much the same way as the Ashante treat the unworthy in their society. The idea is an attractive one and the fact that many of these bodies were weighed down with stones (to prevent the spirits rising?) adds some support. An alternative possibility that should not be overlooked, however, is that these bodies were sacrifices – propitiatory offerings similar to the special animal burials – intended to placate the gods and ensure fertility. Both hypotheses are equally plausible in the circumstances.

The human skulls are rather easier to understand in the context of Celtic society. The head was regarded as the seat of a man's power and ownership of a head meant control over that power. Head hunting was widespread and is well attested in both the archaeological record of the Celts and in Classical literature describing their activities. One quotation from Diodorus Siculus will suffice.

87 *Human skull buried in the top of a pit.*

88 *Infant burial.*

They cut off the heads of enemies slain in battle and attach them to the necks of their horses. The bloodstained spoils they hand over to their attendants and carry off as booty . . . They nail up these first fruits upon their houses . . . They embalm in cedar oil the heads of the most distinguished enemies and preserve them carefully in a chest and display them with pride to strangers saying that for this head one of their ancestors or his father, or the man himself, refused the offer of a large sum of money.

Here, then, is one practice which could have led to the collection and deposition of skulls, but

89 *Diagram to show how a human pelvis was hacked from the corpse before burial. A and B are two sides of one of the femur heads; C is the other femur head; D shows the sword slashes on the pelvis.*

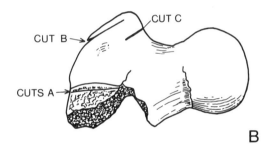

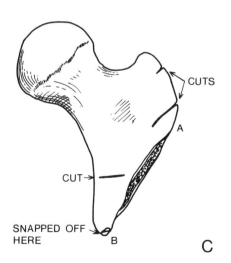

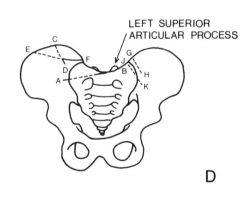

other models are equally possible. In some societies the heads of ancestors were cherished and kept about the house as an act of piety. There is nothing to distinguish the Danebury skulls as belonging to enemies rather than ancestors.

It remains to consider the dismembered bodies. Various explanations are possible but the one which best fits all the available data is that the rites of passage of the dead involved a period when the bodies were exposed for the flesh to rot before the remains were collected for burial. Such proceedings are well attested in the anthropological literature in many parts of the world and embody the belief that there is an interval between life and death when the soul still hovers, formless and stateless, about the corpse. This liminal period ends when the soul finally transcends to the land of the ancestors, a passage often marked by feasting and the ritual processing of the remains of the corpse, usually culminating in burial. In some societies there is a strong link between rites of this kind and agricultural fertility rituals, the final burial being seen as an act of propitiation ensuring the continuity of life for the whole community.

The observed evidence from Danebury fits well with such a system of beliefs. The dead, worthy to be afforded normal burial, would be taken to a sacred site, presumably outside the fort, and the bodies exposed for a time, during which the flesh would begin to rot and carnivores would move in. Then, after the approved period, the remains would be brought back to the fort, some parts being buried in pits as propitiatory offerings while other elements, such as skulls and long bones, were selected for special treatment possibly connected with an ancestor cult. The story is entirely plausible and may even approximate to what really happened, but as with so much of archaeological interpretation it is necessary to sound the warning that other explanations are always possible.

We may be witnessing nothing more than the results of clearing up after periodic bouts of killing (or plague) or the aftermath of human sacrifice or even cannibalism – we will never know for certain. All that can be said is that a complex ritual involving excarnation followed by propitiatory burial neatly contains the observed facts and conforms to a recognized pattern of human behaviour.

Social structure

Discussion of the burial data has introduced some of the intricacies of social structure and this difficult but fascinating subject must now be addressed. One approach to the problem is to look at the way in which one of the well recorded Celtic societies worked and to see if there is any possible correlation with the data from Wessex. Ample documentary evidence survives of the arrangement of Irish society in the early part of the first millennium AD, untouched by the heavy hand of Roman imperialism. The quite startling similarities between Ireland and the situation in Gaul much earlier, in the middle of the first century BC, at the moment when Caesar was beginning his conquest, confirm the belief that Celtic society was organized in a broadly similar manner across space and time.

The basic unit of organization in Ireland was the *derbfine* or extended family – a family of four generations, being the descendants of a common great-grandfather. Land was owned by the *derbfine*, not by any particular individual. A number of family units of this kind made up the *tuath* or tribe. *Tuath* was, in fact, the term used for both the social unit and the land which it occupied. It was ruled by a king (*rĭ*) who was bound by ties of personal allegiance to a higher king (*ruiri*) who in turn owed allegiance to a paramount king (*rĭ ruirech*).

The *tuath* was rigorously stratified into a number of social classes, the distinctions between which were carefully maintained. Below the king were the noble warriors (*flaithi*) and the skilled men (*oes dána*) who included the craftsmen, poets, lawyers, teachers and the keepers of the tribal histories and genealogies, all enjoying the patronage of the *flaithi* and the *rĭ*. Further down the social scale were the ordinary freemen (*grád féne*) who worked the land and paid a tithe of their produce to the king.

Most of the freemen placed themselves in a state of voluntary clientship to the nobles and were known as *céle*. Clientship was an important social mechanism which created an effective system for the redistribution of produce. In its simplest form the noble provided cattle for the use of his client in return for a rent made up of an agreed tithe of products and of service. Since it was in the interests of the noble to keep a wary eye on his wealth, the client enjoyed his lord's protection. The Irish law tracts provide considerable detail about the different systems of clientship and laid down precise details of the rent a lord would be eligible to receive. One example of such an agreement involved the use of 24 cows. For this the client had to pay annually a fat cow, a salted pig, eight sacks of malt, a sack of wheat and three handfuls of rush candles. This kind of system was both simple and effective. It meant that the warrior class was freed from the burden of food production but it also gave the nobility the responsibility of protecting those engaged in the everyday chores of cultivation and herding. The skilled men, through the patronage of the nobility, were also free to practise their arts without having to till the fields and guard the flocks. It was this kind of society that Caesar had in mind when he wrote:

> Everywhere in Gaul there are only two classes of men who are of any account or consideration. The common people are treated almost as slaves, never venture to act on their own initiative and are not consulted on any subject. Most of them, crushed by debt or heavy taxation or the oppression of more powerful persons bind themselves to serve men of rank, who exercise over them all the rights that masters have over slaves. The two privileged classes are the Druids and the knights.

Caesar's view was evidently somewhat jaundiced but behind the bias and misunderstandings all the elements we have described of the Irish system can be detected. He goes on to outline the activities of the knights:

> When their services are required in some war that has broken out . . . they all take the field surrounded by their servants and retainers of whom each Knight has a greater or lesser number according to his birth or fortune. The possession of such a following is the only criterion of position and power that they recognize.

This provides a clear indication of the power of the nobles to call on their clients for war service when need arose, the status of the noble being reflected in the number of his clients.

Another system of great importance to the stability of Celtic society was fosterage. The sons and daughters of lesser nobles were sent to the homes of more exalted men to be brought up and taught the necessary skills of life. Bonds of fosterage were very strong. Foster parents could look to the support of foster children in their old age, while children brought up in the same families would retain a bond of mutual respect and assistance throughout life. Clientship, fosterage and marriage were the three principal mechanisms by which society retained a semblance of order and stability.

All this takes us some way from the Iron Age of Wessex and from the archaeology of Danebury, and it might reasonably be asked whether generalizations about Celtic society are of any relevance at all to these matters. It would, indeed, be quite improper to try to impose the details of an Irish social system of the first millennium AD, or a Gaulish pattern of Caesar's time, on central southern Britain in the late first millennium BC, but since these models offer us the closest insight it is possible to gain into broadly contemporary Celtic society, it is worth considering how they compare with the available archaeological data.

The first question it is necessary to approach is the relationship of Danebury to the farmsteads of the surrounding countryside. The farmsteads vary in size and form but are usually ditched enclosures 1–2ha (2–5 acres) in extent containing evidence of houses, granaries and storage pits together with a range of domestic debris suggesting that the craft activities practised were similar to those found in the hillfort. Superficially there is little to distinguish them except their size, but if we move beyond the simple presence and absence approach and begin to think in terms of quantifying various aspects of the record then significant differences begin to emerge. In the first place Danebury has about twenty times the storage capacity of an average farmstead and this alone must imply a significantly different status. It has already been mentioned that of the products brought into the fort, some of the grain was grown on land well outside the range of farming activities based on the fort itself, while there is sufficient evidence to suggest (but not to prove) that surplus wool was brought in for weaving, which was undertaken on a large scale. The stone weights show that precise measurement was being carried out and the briquetage is indicative of at least one rare commodity – salt – being imported in quantity for redistribution. Evidence of this kind, considered in some detail in the last chapter, led to the suggestion that developed

109

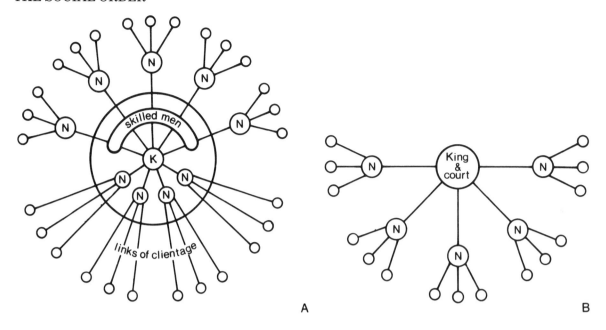

A

B

K king
N noble
O freemen farmers

90 *Diagram to give some tentative ideas of the kind of social structure which may have been in operation. A assumes the king, his followers and some nobles reside in the fort; B assumes that only the king and his followers are resident.*

hillforts, like Danebury, performed central-place functions, serving as redistribution centres for their territories.

If this is explained in simple social terms it would imply that a tithe of the products of the countryside – grain and wool – was passing into the hillfort, while in return raw materials and manufactured goods were passing out to the farmsteads. The situation could, therefore, be one in which a clientage relationship linked the hillfort dwellers to the farmers of the country-side. Beyond this it is more difficult to venture with any degree of assurance.

One possible model would be to see the hill-fort as the residence of the king and his extended family, together with the specialist craftsmen and other skilled men of the tribe (**90**). The estimated population of 200–350 at Danebury would not be at all excessive for such a community. In support of this model can be mentioned the existence of the shrines, perhaps reflecting the presence of a religious elite, the ample evidence of bronze and iron working, pointing to craft activity on a large scale, and the weights suggesting control of measure-ment. The argument has the advantage of at least being plausible. To pursue it further we would need to ask whether any of the hillfort community was involved in food production. The close physical relationship of the field sys-tems to the fort defences might suggest that this was so, and if it is correct to argue that the kraals around the fort were used in times of lambing and calving then some degree of agri-cultural base must be accepted. There is noth-ing inherently difficult in supposing that members of the king's extended family were involved in agricultural work, but it is more likely that the fields were worked and the flocks and herds tended by the lower ranks of unfree clients or by slaves. If the provision of kraal space fairly reflects the size of the live-stock population then, in this model, the king would be a very wealthy man.

If the hillfort was the residence of king and retinue, the larger 'farms' should be seen as the residences of the noble families, the smaller enclosures and open settlements being the homes of the lower ranks of the client farmers.

This is to some extent supported by the archaeological evidence in that the larger enclosures, like Little Woodbury and Gussage All Saints, had considerable storage capacity. Moreover several of them produced elaborate bronze fittings from horse harnesses suggesting exalted status, and at Gussage there is clear evidence of a skilled smith at work making many sets of horse gear. Lower down the scale there is a range of quite modest enclosures with far more limited storage capacity.

If the nobility lived in the large enclosures of Little Woodbury type, they, like the hillforts, must have retained their agricultural base. Linear ditch systems, suitable for controlling cattle, are associated with many of them and field systems are integral with the enclosures. But again this could easily be explained in terms of unfree clients or slaves undertaking the actual agricultural and herding work on land belonging to the noble's family. A king would have exacted tribute from nobles in the same way as the noble relied on his clients.

There is nothing, then, too difficult in supposing that the social system in operation in the Wessex Iron Age conformed to a generalized Celtic model and that the hillforts represented the settlements of the elite, but of the intricacies of the system little can be known. The possibility that nobles also occupied the fort should not be overlooked nor need it be supposed that the aristocracy remained in one place all year round: these, however, are questions well beyond the scope of archaeology.

An alternative interpretation is also worth exploring – that the fort was a communal structure containing the religious focus of the polity and providing for its surplus storage needs but was not a place of permanent elite residence. If so it would be necessary to argue that the houses and other streets in the peripheral zone behind the rampart were used only as temporary residences during part of the year when a segment of the society congregated within the defences for social or religious reasons, equivalent perhaps to an annual fair. To explore this possibility further it is necessary to search for evidence of seasonality in data: this study is now in progress and when complete may well resolve the question finally.

The annual fair was an important event in the Celtic world. In Irish society the principal fair (oenach) was of provincial status and held close to the chief stronghold. It was attended by all the tribes in the province and lasted several days while public business was enacted, entertainments enjoyed and goods exchanged. Just as there were three levels of kingship so were there three types of oenach. The annual fair is an essential component of any social system in which rural communities lived closely together. The need to meet in tribal and intertribal gatherings to re-establish social boundaries and social links was of paramount importance. It has pervaded European society from the earliest times and is still in evidence even today, though in a much modified form, in our bank holiday fairs held on common land.

One explanation for the 'ritual' pits surrounding Danebury Hill in the early first millennium is that they defined a place of social gatherings, and the density of Neolithic long barrows and Bronze Age round barrows might suggest that Danebury Hill had been a focal location much earlier. If these speculations are correct the use of the hilltop for the annual oenach in the Iron Age would be merely an extension of a tradition which continued, albeit sporadically, to the time of Henry VII when the last organized fairs were held on the hill. Fairs of this kind could well have been the occasion for propitiatory offerings to be made to the gods to ensure fertility or for the exposed corpses of the dead to be consigned to the earth.

If the oenach was the way in which society maintained its precarious balance by large-scale interactions, the feast was the means for the smaller group to define its levels of friendship and allegiance. Various Classical writers offer vivid details of Celtic feasts. They were noisy drunken affairs but circumscribed by rigid rules of behaviour:

> When a large number dine together they sit around in a circle with the most influential man in the centre like the leader of a chorus . . . Beside him sits the host and next, on either side, the others in order of distinction. Their shieldsmen stand behind them while their spearmen are seated in a circle on the opposite side and feast in common like their lords. [Athenaeus quoting Posidonius.]

Diodorus Siculus, also quoting Posidonius, adds further colour:

> . . . beside them are hearths blazing with fire with cauldrons and spits containing large pieces of meat. Brave warriors they honour with the finest pieces of meat.

91 *Iron cauldron hooks used to suspend the cauldron over the fire.*

As already mentioned, the doling out of the various joints often gave rise to disputes which sometimes led to outright conflict. Salt and fresh pork, beef, milk, bread and wheaten beer prepared with honey are all mentioned as the usual fare, and to enliven the occasion there were bards who sang to the accompaniment of musical instruments resembling lyres – sometimes they sang eulogies, sometimes satires. Popular performances would have included the folk tales embodying the genealogies and oral traditions of the tribe. Rousing stuff to make men proud and to make them feel part of a common brotherhood.

The raucous self-indulgence of it all, the boasting and the latent violence are not difficult to picture with the help of the classical texts, but standing on a bare hilltop in the pouring rain watching the mud wash down over a freshly excavated chalk floor emphasizes the enormous gap between life as it was led and the sparseness of the archaeological record. But there is the hut floor and there the central fireplace and just outside are midden deposits with remains of the joints of pork and beef. And just occasionally, surprising and reassuring discoveries are made, like a hoard of iron work found in 1979 containing the two beautifully forged hooks to hang the cauldron over the fires (**91**) and two iron spits to skewer the meat. Who, seeing the hoard and reading Diodorus' account of a feast, could really doubt the relevance of the classical accounts of Celtic society to the Iron Age of Wessex?

10

The end of Danebury

In about 100 BC or soon after, when the defences of Danebury were at their most elaborate and dumps of sling stones were arranged ready for use close to the main entrance, the great inner gate was burnt down. Thereafter much of the interior was abandoned and soon became derelict. In the quarry hollows behind the ramparts tools and horse gear were left on the floors of houses to be covered by layers of silt washed down from the interior. The picture is one of sudden destruction followed by abandonment.

Two of the latest pits on the site, both quite close to the gate, contained the mutilated remains of 21 human bodies, some represented by only parts of the corpse. Men, women and children were included, ranging in age from four to 45. The remains seem to have been thrown into the open pits and left there until, by frost and water action, the pit sides began to crumble and the holes gradually filled with silt and rubble. Burial of partly dismembered corpses was a long established ritual at Danebury (see above, pp. 103–4), but these two deposits differ from the others in that the number of bodies involved was exceptionally large and both came at the very end of the main period of occupation, after which the site was virtually abandoned. One possibility is that they are the results of a clearing up operation after a massacre, but a more likely explanation, in view of the burial tradition, is that excarnated bodies were gathered together and quickly disposed of before the site was abandoned.

There are two ways to approach the problems posed by the end of Danebury, first by considering what was happening locally to society in the immediately preceding period, and second by taking a wider view and looking at the socio-political changes in south-eastern Britain and its approaches.

Population pressure

One of the most important single factors affecting Iron Age society in southern Britain was growth in population. Actual figures are impossible to produce but field surveys in various parts of the country have shown that the number of late Iron Age sites had greatly increased compared with the earlier period and if this can be taken to reflect an increase in population over a period of 400 years or so, then by the second century BC we are forced to accept that the population density had risen to very considerable proportions. We may even be witnessing a rare case of an exponential increase. A rise in population, once it reaches the holding capacity of the land will cause stress. That this was so is surely demonstrated by the very existence of hillforts. The growth of massively defended enclosures, with increasing emphasis on military strength, and the fact that many of them show more than one phase of gate burning, are striking indications of stress. It can also be suggested on anthropological grounds that an increase in propitiatory burials is another symptom of tension: just such an increase is to be found at Danebury.

The hillfort-dominated landscape of Wessex very probably represents a society in which the population level was fluctuating around the maximum holding capacity of a landscape being progressively depleted. Social systems had developed that held the situation in a state of unstable equilibrium, but warfare increased and with it the power of essentially non-productive war leaders. It was a system that had within itself the germs of its own destruction and when

113

external factors began to make themselves felt the old system collapsed.

Roman influence

To understand these external factors the story must move, briefly, to southern France. For centuries Greek colonists had been established around the Mediterranean shores of France and Spain trading with the barbarians of the hinterland. Rome kept well clear at first but eventually, in 124 BC, the Roman armies moved into southern Gaul and annexed the territory setting up the Roman Province. In the wake of the Roman armies, came entrepreneurs eager to get rich through a subtle blend of trade and exploitation.

There already existed a long established network of trade routes across barbarian Gaul both overland and by river and along the Atlantic sea-ways. The Romans would not have been aware in any detail of the intricacies of the sailing patterns and indeed when local sailors were questioned they were not very forthcoming with information. It was probably for this reason that Publius Crassus set sail at the beginning of the first century BC to shadow the coastal traders in order to learn where tin supplies were to be had. After initial difficulties he was successful and returned triumphant to give details of the routes to Roman entrepreneurs eager to exploit this potentially profitable new market.

Something of the nature of the trade pattern can be gleaned from the writings of Cicero, who as a famous orator was asked to speak in the defence of M. Fronteius one time propraetor of the Province. Fronteius, like so many of his kind, was accused of extortion and was brought to trial. In his long speech Cicero throws an interesting sidelight on early trade. It appears that great quantities of Italian wine were offloaded at Narbonne and moved across to the Garonne at Toulouse and as each amphora passed through a town or staging post the locals charged a portage tax on it – after all, Cicero said, this did not much matter because it was being sold to the barbarians! Another writer tells us that the Gauls loved wine so much that they were prepared to trade a slave for a single amphora.

All this is a long way from Danebury but it is, indirectly, highly relevant. What was happening was that an ancient system of exchange, embedded in a network of long established social relationships, was suddenly being transformed into a capitalist-based system of trade motivated by highly efficient Roman entrepreneurs for personal profit. The extent and intensity of the Roman-inspired imports can be appreciated by looking at the distribution of the characteristic amphorae (called Dressel type 1A) in which the Italian wine was exported. They cluster along the Atlantic sea-ways concentrating in Brittany and in central southern Britain. Several wrecks along the French coast and another one reported near the Isle of Wight give a further insight into the traffic.

It is now abundantly clear that the principal port-of-call in Britain at this time was at Hengistbury Head on the Dorset coast, dominating the fine anchorage of Christchurch harbour with its river routes, the Avon and Stour, leading into the heart of densely occupied Wessex. Excavations have shown that Hengistbury was the place where ships leaving the Armorican coast landed with their cargoes of Italian wine, fine Breton pottery and blocks of raw glass, and no doubt took aboard some of the commodities for which Britain was famous – its metals, slaves, hides and hunting dogs. There is, in fact, ample evidence of the metal trade at Hengistbury in the form of Mendip lead, copper/silver ore from the fringes of southern Dartmoor and local iron from the headland itself. From the sheer quantity of material found, there can be little doubt that manufacturing and trading activity was intense and it appears to have developed quite suddenly.

Standing back from the miscellany of evidence, both archaeological and documentary, it is valid to say that Roman entrepreneurial activity about 100 BC seems quickly to have opened up new markets with the barbarian west and in particular with southern Britain. A demand for commodities, such as slaves, for the Roman consumer market and the availability of ample supplies of prestige products like wine for the local aristocracy cannot have failed to have had a dramatic and dislocating effect on native communities, in much the same way as the American slave trade caused catastrophic change among the communities of west Africa in more recent times. This may have been one of the prime factors causing the collapse of the socio-economic system represented by the hillforts of central southern Britain.

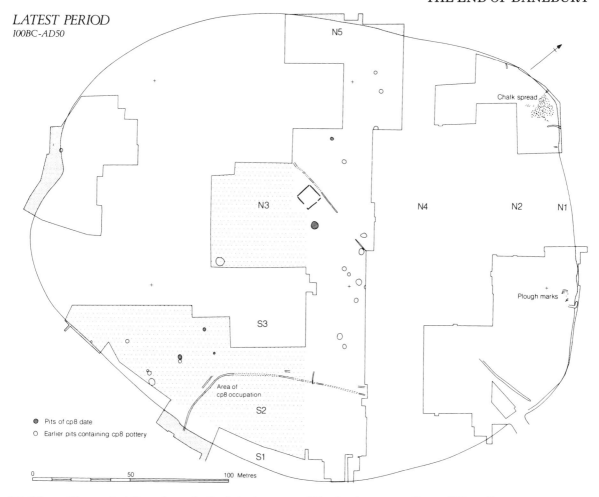

LATEST PERIOD
100BC–AD50

N5

Chalk spread

N3

N4 N2 N1

Plough marks

S3

Area of
cp8 occupation

S2

S1

● Pits of cp8 date
○ Earlier pits containing cp8 pottery

0   50   100 Metres

92 *The settlement at Danebury in its latest phase.*

The Atlantic trade with Hengistbury was very short lived. Taking the broadest view, it began about 100 BC or a little before, and lasted for about 50 years, after which there is evidence of decline. The first century BC was a time of rapidly changing socio-political alignments. Caesar's conquest of Gaul (58–51 BC) completely changed the political geography of western Europe with the result that trade along the Atlantic sea-ways declined as the Rhine commercial corridor took over. The effect was to focus trade with the Roman world on eastern Britain – Essex and Hertfordshire – where new centres of wealth emerged, leaving Wessex and the west to develop in relative isolation after having adapted socially and economically to the new reality of the close proximity of the Roman commercial world.

The last occupation of Danebury
Returning now to Danebury, intense occupation seems to have come to a sudden end some time about 100 BC, when many other hillforts show similar signs of disruption. In the century and a half between this event and the even greater social upheaval caused by the Roman invasion of AD 43, Danebury continued to be occupied (**92**). Perhaps the most dramatic evidence for this is at the east gate where the road remained in use and was worn into a considerable hollow way long after the last gate posts had been burnt. The surface was metalled with pebbles and in some places the ruts of the cart wheels could still be seen. Clearly, intensive traffic was passing into and out of the fort. What is surprising is that the wear on the road surface was even more considerable in this latest period than in the preceding times. One reason may be that it was not regularly maintained and surfaced after 100 BC and therefore

wore more rapidly, but an alternative possibility is that cattle were now being driven into the enclosure on a regular basis causing a more intense pattern of wear than had previously been experienced.

There is some supporting evidence for this latter view. The old quarry hollows on the north and east sides of the enclosure, where previously there had been closely packed houses, now began to silt up with a chalky silt, which reached a maximum thickness of about 1m (3ft). The consistency of the silt, with a high chalk content, and the absence of any evidence of internal stratigraphy, strongly suggests that the layer developed very quickly. This could have happened only if the adjacent higher parts of the interior of the enclosure had been kept free of binding vegetation so that rain could wash the unprotected soil down into the quarry hollow. Of the two ways in which these conditions could have been created – ploughing and the constant breaking of the soil by animals' hooves – the latter seems the more likely in the circumstances, though some evidence of ploughing has been discovered dating to an early stage before a great depth of silt had accumulated.

This outline fits quite well with what is known of occupation in the rest of the fort. Immediately after the destruction of *c.* 100 BC a group of pottery can be defined which we call ceramic phase 8 (**93**). It owes much to the traditions of the preceding period, with bead-rimmed jars decorated with shallow tooling, but the forms are different, with rather sharper and more tightly moulded profiles brought about by the vessels being finished on a slow-turning potter's wheel. Some of the jars are so well made that they were probably entirely wheel-turned. This new technological innovation brought with it several new forms, such as jars with elegantly moulded pedestal bases and bowls with well defined necks and cordons at the junction of the neck and shoulder. Both types, though clearly of local manufacture, owe much in their inspiration to forms imported from north-west France to Hengistbury Head in the period *c.* 100–50 BC and there can be little reasonable doubt that the cross-Channel trade contacts, developing at this time, were responsible for introducing a range of new ideas into central southern Britain. One of these, the potter's wheel, was widely adopted.

Another new element to appear at Danebury

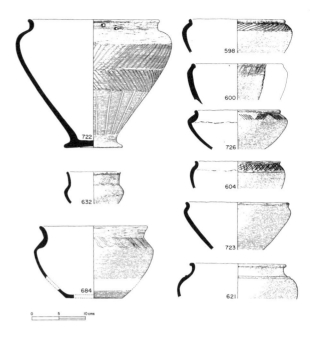

93 *Pottery of the first century* BC.

at this time is Italian wine, or more correctly sherds of the amphorae in which the wine was imported. Though not numerous, amphora sherds have been found directly associated with pottery of ceramic phase 8, providing additional evidence of a link with the coastal regions where the imports arrived. Put in its broader context there is nothing particularly unusual about this assemblage – it simply represents a stage of transition in which the effects of the newly developed systems of long distance trade were beginning to make themselves felt. Wine amphorae, presumably with their contents, were finding their way to a number of settlements of varying status either as the result of gift exchange or in the wake of some kind of commercial transaction.

Little can be said of the Danebury community at this time except that it was very limited in size compared with what had gone before. Occupation seems to have concentrated in the centre of the site close to the 'shrines', one or two of which could still have been standing. Only a few pits were definitely open at this time; elsewhere the limited quantity of pottery found came from the topmost layers of old pits already largely filled.

In the decades immediately following the destruction in *c.* 100 BC, we must, therefore, visualize the entrance road leading past the

charred remains of the old gate through derelict and overgrown ramparts to a clearing
around the old shrines where there was a small
community, perhaps a single family, still living.
It is tempting to believe that only the priests
remained.

Whether or not the ceramic phase 8 occupation continued for long we will never know but
by the last 50 years before the Roman invasion
of AD 43 the situation had changed. It was
probably at this time that a fence, or hedge,
with a ditch in front was set out across the fort
dividing off the northern half of the defended
enclosure. Since it was here that the evidence
for trampling by animals was found, it may be
that the area became a kraal for livestock set
aside from the rest of the fort in which the
contemporary farm was built.

The homestead was sited against the back of
the rampart on the southern side of the fort and
seems to have been associated with a drainage
ditch. No pits were dug and while some post-
holes can be shown to be of this date, no
building plan can be made out. The associated
pottery (called ceramic phase 9) is more sophisticated than that of the preceding period: wheel
turning was now general, a range of imported
Gallo-Belgic platters was copied in local fabrics
and a few flagons – probably imports – surviving now only as fragments, were brought to the
site.

Other finds of this late period include simple
bronze brooches of safety-pin type and it may
be to this period that the three Celtic coins from
Danebury belong (94). One of Gallo-Belgic C
type was found high up in the silt of one of the
hornwork ditches, one of King Verica came
from the entrance forecourt, while the third,
belonging to the Durotriges – the tribe
occupying Dorset – was discovered somewhere
in the interior in the nineteenth century. More
recently a group of 70 Celtic coins was picked
up from the field just outside the east entrance,
covering the period 50 BC-AD 50. It is possible
that they represent the site of a market or a
shrine (or both) sited outside the old defences.
Together the collection is interesting in that it
reflects the continued use of the site in the
immediate pre-Roman period, but gives no real
indication of the status of the occupants.

That the old hillfort should be used by a small
community at this late stage is not particularly
surprising since the earthworks were a convenient place within which to build a settlement

94 *Iron Age coins from Danebury: a Gallo-
Belgic C; b Verica; c Durotrigian. (Scale × 2.)*

and it is even possible that some thread of
continuity of ownership was involved, with the
later occupants being descendants of the earlier
chieftains or kings. But other explanations are
equally possible. Could it not be that the settlement was that of the resident religious hierarchy who stayed to maintain the sanctity of
the place? A fort occupied for 500 years, with a
complex of shrines at the centre, is hardly
likely to have lost its religious significance to
the community even though its political and
economic functions may have wasted away.

The abandonment of developed hillforts, or at
least a dramatic change in the intensity and
nature of the occupation, some time about or
soon after 100 BC, seems to have affected the
whole of the territory of the Atrebates covering
large parts of southern Britain from Sussex
westwards into Wiltshire and Dorset, though at
some of the western forts, such as Maiden
Castle, Hod Hill and South Cadbury, there is
clear evidence of reuse at the time of the

Roman invasion in AD 43. Within the territory of the Atrebates two new centres developed, one on the south coast at Selsey just south of Chichester and the other at Silchester on the northern border of Hampshire. Both became major economic foci where coins were minted and through which, presumably, external trade was articulated. Another centre of this kind may have developed at Winchester but the evidence is ambiguous.

Below these in status it is possible to recognize a category of small, roughly circular multivallate enclosures, like Chisbury or Boscombe Down West (Wiltshire), and Suddern Farm (Hampshire) not far west of Danebury. Very little is known of these sites but the scale of their earthworks suggests a degree of coercive power appropriate to a minor chieftain. The trial excavation at Suddern Farm confirmed the massiveness of the ditches and produced an assemblage of the first century BC and early

first century AD appropriate to an elite residence. Do such sites represent an element of continuity with the old social order? This is a question that must await a fuller programme of excavation.

Finally, in the countryside, there seems to have been comparatively little change in settlement location. Many of the old farmsteads continued in use but the large enclosures of Little Woodbury and Gussage type were not kept up. Some were abandoned altogether; others continued to be occupied but with smaller enclosures, often several together, replacing the more straggling earlier settlement. Clearly, there were reorientations in rural society and in economy but their meaning is obscure. It is all part of the great upheaval that left the old hillforts – some of them centres of prestige and power for more than 400 years – derelict ruins, reminders of a social order now past.

11

Aftermath: fairs and rabbits

The Romans

In AD 43 the Roman legions landed in Kent to begin their conquest of Britain, a process which was to take 40 years. The south-east was very rapidly secured and within three years a frontier zone had been created based on a road from Exeter to Lincoln. South of the Thames the conquest was in the hands of the *Legio II Augusta* under the command of Vespasian (later to become emperor). It would seem that the Atrebates of west Sussex, Hampshire, Berkshire and Wiltshire offered no significant resistance and may indeed have become the allies of Rome from the outset. The last of the Atrebatic kings, Verica, had fled to Rome for help, and in the aftermath of the conquest we find a native king, Cogidubnus, possibly Verica's heir, showered with honours by the new administration.

The Durotriges, on the other hand, opposed the Roman armies and their opposition was forcefully and violently overcome. More than twenty native hillforts were stormed by Vespasian's troops leaving in their wake dead bodies and devastation of the kind so dramatically recorded at Maiden Castle and Spettisbury where evidence of massacre and hasty burial has come to light. In the years immediately following, insecurity necessitated the quartering of Roman troops in forts throughout Durotrigian territory and even as late as AD 60–1, when Queen Boudica was leading a rebellion in the east of Britain, the Durotriges were too dangerous to leave unguarded. Evidence of a local uprising was found at South Cadbury where slaughtered bodies were left unburied in the gateway.

Against this background central Wessex seems to have been quite peaceful. Occasional pieces of military equipment, like a spur found on Cleave Hill, 4km (2½ miles) east of Danebury, simply reflect the passing of the army, but there is no evidence of resistance and Danebury may even have been by-passed.

In the four centuries or so of Roman occupation the hill was little used. A coin of the Emperor Vespasian and a handful of Roman potsherds are all that survive of the period, suggesting sporadic visits perhaps by shepherds. Just outside the fort, the ridge approaching the east gate was scarred with hollow trackways leading from the open downs towards the bridging point of the Test at Stockbridge. Some of these old drove ways may date back to Roman times when the landscape around was being heavily exploited by small farming estates centred around Roman villas. Many of these villas are known and several of them occupied the site of pre-Roman farms, suggesting a strong degree of continuity. There is nothing incongruous in the idea that the villa owners were the direct descendants of the Iron Age farmers whose surplus produce, instead of being given in tribute to a king and dissipated in feasts and other kinds of social display, as was the case in the pre-Roman period, was now being paid as tax to the Roman government and was being used to acquire such luxurious trappings of Roman life as masonry buildings, mosaics, central heating and baths. The roads were better and life was more comfortable and peaceful but little else had changed.

Danebury's last defences

There still remains the problem of Danebury's last defences. At some undefined stage the ditch was partially redug in a rather clever way. Instead of digging out the fill of the old

119

V-shaped ditch, the new defenders simply trimmed back the upper sides to make them vertical and dumped the spoil into the hollow above the existing silting. The result was, with a minimum of effort, to create a wide, flat-bottomed obstacle 11m (36ft) wide and more than 2m (6½ft) deep. Anyone attacking the fort would have been particularly vulnerable when crossing the ditch and the vertical sides would have made it difficult for them to scramble back out, not least because their backs would have been exposed to the fire of defenders on the rampart. The recutting of the ditch in this manner was taken around the outer hornworks at the east gate and the hornworks were themselves heightened. The date of this work is totally unknown. It could belong to the last stage of the Iron Age or, more likely, the immediate post-Roman period when many of the old hillforts were brought back into use. There is no direct evidence for intensive occupation at this time in Danebury but sherds of coarse, grass-tempered pottery, indicative of a fifth- or sixth-century date, have been found unstratified in the interior. Thus, while there is no compelling reason to date the last defences to the sub-Roman period, the context is both plausible and attractive: if accepted Danebury emerges as a stronghold again in the Celtic twilight!

Danebury in the Middle Ages and later

Of the Middle Ages there is little to be said. Dunbury, as it was called, dominated the skyline but people chose to live in the river valleys, in villages strung out along the river Wallop or the river Test, while at Stockbridge, where a convenient causeway with bridges was constructed across the flood plain of the Test, a small town developed on the road between Winchester and Salisbury. All this while Danebury lay abandoned, visited only by sheep and shepherds. It may, however, have been used once a year as a rural fair for, in the sixteenth century Henry VII granted a charter which permitted a fair to be held on St Margaret's Day (20 July). While this may have been the instigation of something quite new, it is not impossible that the charter simply legalized a local tradition. Rural fairs were a vital means of communication in the Middle Ages when long distance travel to towns like Salisbury or Winchester would have been quite out of the question for most of the population. Like the annual gatherings of the Celts, the fair was a time to meet people and exchange gossip, to make deals, to buy and sell and to relax. It is particularly fitting that the local fair should have been held on the spot where similar activities had taken place, albeit sporadically, for the previous 2000 years.

By the beginning of the seventeenth century the fair was defunct but the hill had taken on a new function as a rabbit warren for which there is both documentary and archaeological evidence. The documentary evidence consists of a compilation of papers relating to a tithe dispute in the parish of Nether Wallop. In its present form the document is eighteenth century but it contains a copy of an account written in 1678 about the situation earlier that century.

> Dunbury-hill . . . was anciently and till since the memory of man a warren and let to several tennants at rack rents and was entire to itself and (not a sheep common) had a lodge in it. Only since the rabbits were destroyed they have fed their sheep there, and when it was a warren the sheep many times went over it and not questioned because the warreners' rabbits trespassed as much on their sheep-down.

The account goes on to say that about 60 years previously (i.e. c. 1618) between 6 and 12 acres of the hill within the defences close to the lodge were 'broken-up'. A second period of breaking took place later in 1655 when the parson sued for a tithe of all the newly cultivated land in the Summer Assizes of 1656.

The picture, then, is fairly clear: until the early years of the seventeenth century the hill had been occupied by a rabbit warren guarded by a resident warrener. But the warren became defunct and twice during the seventeenth century the interior of the fort was dug over to improve the soil, presumably to provide higher quality pasture for sheep.

The breeding of rabbits was an important part of the rural medieval economy because a plentiful supply ensured both meat and an additional income from the skins. It was far simpler to create artificial warrens, which would encourage breeding and provide a greater control over the snaring, than to rely on trapping in the wild. Sometimes the warrens were of artificial banks of earth called 'pillow mounds' but at Danebury more sophisticated warrens were created by actually digging the burrows in the solid chalk and filling them with soil or vegetation, or possibly even boarding them over, before putting the topsoil back.

There were two principal types. The first consisted of parallel trenches joined at intervals, or a single spine trench, with others joining at right angles. The second was more complicated: a long trench was dug in the bottom of a broader slot and from the sides of the trench, at intervals, rabbit-sized burrows were bored through the chalk to the surface (**95**). The overriding concept was simple: rabbits introduced into such a system would live quite happily in the burrows made for them, using the entrances and exits provided. The warrener would, of course, know where all the exits were and when rabbits were required would block all but one at which he would set his nets or snares. Nothing was left to chance, but it was particularly pleasing to find that in some places where warrens were dug through the tops of old Iron Age pits, the looser soil allowed the more adventurous beasts to branch out for themselves creating their own exits, from which a few must surely have escaped!

The warren's lodge mentioned in the text lay in the centre of the fort close to the highest point. It was a simple affair built of cob walls on a flint and cob base and roofed with clay tiles. The floor was of flint cobbles. There was little evidence of comfort and comparatively little domestic debris to indicate the activities which went on.

The seventeenth-century improvements – the 'breaking up' of the Down – were everywhere in evidence in the form of close-spaced parallel trenches, some 60cm (2ft) wide and 5–7m (16–23ft) long, dug into the surface of the natural chalk. The trenches were two spade-widths wide and in many cases it was possible to trace the actual marks made by the round-ended spades. The purpose of this activity was twofold: to increase the depth of the soil and to turn fresh chalk up into the humus to counteract the acidity of the soil which would tend to develop, even on chalkland, if pasture was left undisturbed for a long period. By first throwing the topsoil from one trench into the bottom of the adjacent one left open and then shovelling broken chalk from the trench on top of the redeposited topsoil both purposes were achieved. Soil improvement schemes of this kind, though enormously labour-intensive,

95 *Rabbit-warren substructure excavated in 1981.*

were popular in the seventeenth and eighteenth centuries.

The improved downland supported sheep throughout the seventeenth, eighteenth and early nineteenth centuries but rabbits continued to run wild and even after the hilltop was planted with trees in the middle of the nineteenth century the rabbits continued in occupation. It was, after all, the digging out of rabbits in 1859 that led to the visit of Sir Augustus Franks and the first archaeological exploration with which the first chapter began.

A long association with a single site – and a place as sympathetic and evocative as Danebury – cannot fail to create a feeling of respect and of love. We have watched Danebury change over the years from the silent mysterious beech wood of the late 1960s, through the devastation of the mid-1970s, to its present state, with established trees and new growth attempting to achieve a harmony. Throughout this time we have explored it with care and have come to learn something of the people who formed it and used it. Inevitably some of the mystery has gone, to be replaced by a new fascination for what we have learnt and a deep humility when we realize how little we yet understand. Our knowledge of the past will always be incomplete, our understanding will always be an approximation to the truth. Iron Age studies have come a long way in a hundred years since people like Pitt Rivers began to ask questions and design excavations to answer them. Danebury has made its contribution.

Further reading

A great deal has been written on the Iron Age in general and on the specific themes explored in this book. In the paragraphs below some guidance is offered to enable the suitably inspired reader to move out into the wider world of Iron Age studies. The lists are very selective but many of the works cited have extensive bibliographies to encourage further forays to be made. The chasing of themes is a very enjoyable pastime – some of us have been lucky enough to make it a lifetime's work.

The Celts at large
Books about the Celtic world are many. The following are a brief selection covering the many aspects from different view points.
Stuart Piggott *The Druids* (Thames & Hudson 1968)
T.G.E. Powell *The Celts* (Thames & Hudson 1958: paperback 1983)
Barry Cunliffe *The Celtic World* (The Bodley Head 1979; Constable 1992)
S. Moscati *The Celts* (Thames & Hudson 1991)

Iron Age society in Britain
There have been several recent books dealing with the topic. The first two deal extensively with the background and have substantial bibliographies. The third offers an account of experimental work carried out on the agricultural background.
D.W. Harding *The Iron Age in Lowland Britain* (Routledge & Kegan Paul 1974)
Barry Cunliffe *Iron Age Communities in Britain* (Routledge & Kegan Paul 1974: third edition 1991)
Peter J. Reynolds *Iron-Age Farm: The Butser Experiment* (Colonnade 1979)

Hillforts in Britain
There is much on offer. The first four are general books giving much detail. Those that follow are about specific sites mentioned.
Margaret Jesson and David Hill *The Iron Age and its Hill-forts* (Southampton 1971)
A.H.A. Hogg *Hill-Forts of Britain* (Hart-Davis, MacGibbon 1975)
D.W. Harding (ed.) *Hillforts: Late Prehistoric Earthworks in Britain and Ireland* (Academic Press 1976)
J. Forde-Johnston *Hillforts of the Iron Age in England and Wales* (Liverpool University Press 1976)
Leslie Alcock *By South Cadbury is that Camelot* (Thames & Hudson 1972)
S.C. Stanford *Croft Ambrey* (Privately printed 1974)
S.C. Stanford *Midsummer Hill: an Iron Age hillfort on the Malverns* (Privately printed 1981)
Barry Cunliffe *Hengistbury Head* (Paul Elek 1978)
Niall Sharples *Maiden Castle* (Batsford/English Heritage 1991)

Books for schools
Suitable up-to-date books are still sadly few but read:
Peter J. Reynolds *Farming in The Iron Age* (Cambridge University Press 1976)
Margaret Herdman *Life in Iron Age Britain* (Harrap 1981)

Publications on Danebury
The definitive reports on the 20 season excavation:
Barry Cunliffe *Danebury: An Iron Age Hillfort in Hampshire:*

Vol. 1. The excavations, 1969–1978: the site
Vol. 2. The excavations, 1969–1978: the finds

Barry Cunliffe and Cynthia Poole *Danebury:
An Iron Age Hillfort in Hampshire:*
Vol. 4. The excavations, 1979–1988: the site
Vol. 5. The excavations, 1979–1988: the finds
(Council for British Archaeology, Vols. 1 and 2,
1984; Vols. 4 and 5, 1991)

Field survey of the Danebury region
Roger Palmer *Danebury: An Iron Age Hillfort
in Hampshire (Vol. 3) An aerial photographic
interpretation of its environs* (Royal Commission on Historic Monuments, England 1984)

Popular guide-book
Barry Cunliffe *Danebury: the story of an Iron
Age Hillfort* (Hampshire County Council 1986)

Places to visit

Danebury is now cared for by Hampshire County Council and can be visited at any time. The fort is a short uphill walk from the car park. A brief explanation of the site is provided in the car park and discrete information plaques enliven the site.

All the finds from Danebury are displayed, together with full-scale reproductions of ramparts and houses, in *The Museum of the Iron Age* at Church Close, Andover, 6 miles from the site (enquiries by telephone: Andover (0264) 66283).

Other hillforts which are easy to visit in the neighbourhood and are in public ownership are Beacon Hill, Burghclere (off the A34 between Whitchurch and Newbury), St Catherine's Hill, Winchester (off the A33 just south of Winchester), and Old Winchester Hill, East Meon (30 minute walk from nearest road).

Glossary

adze Cutting tool hafted like an axe but with the blade at right angles to the haft. Used in woodworking and in pit digging.

amphora Ceramic container used for the transport of wine and oil from the Mediterranean.

ard Simple form of plough. The ard simply breaks the soil while the plough breaks and turns the sod.

Beaker Distinctive pottery vessel common in the period 2200–1700 BC. Usually found accompanying burials.

chape Metal binding for the end of a sword sheath.

colluvium Sands, clays, marls and similar materials moved and deposited by washing down slope often in the periglacial conditions in advance of the ice sheets.

coppice Managed woodland in which trees such as hazel are regularly cut back to encourage rapid new growth providing small timber.

Devonian Geological era during which the Old Red Sandstone was formed.

ethnology The study of recent societies using their material remains as a prime source of evidence.

flotation Technique for separating light organic material such as charred grains from soil.

glauconitic Clay (or pottery made from it) containing the distinctive mineral glauconite.

hanger Woodland growing on steeply sloping land.

loom weight Clay or stone weight used on a vertical loom to keep the vertical threads of wool taut.

lynchet Bank formed at the end of a field by soil which, loosened by the plough, gradually moves down slope by gravity and erosion.

Mesolithic 'Middle stone age'. Roughly 8000–3500 BC when hunter-gatherer communities occupied southern Britain.

Migration period The period of two hundred years or so following the breakdown of Roman rule.

multivallate Defences composed of more than one bank and ditch.

Neolithic 'New stone age' – a period beginning c. 4000 BC and lasting until copper is introduced c. 2200 BC. The first farming communities.

neothermal The period (including the present) following the end of the last ice age c. 10,000 BC.

OD Ordnance Datum. The point regarded as sea-level from which the Ordnance Survey calculates the height of the land.

pannage The running of herds of pigs in woodland where they eat acorns and forage for other foods.

Pleistocene Geological time band corresponding with the last ice ages.

radiocarbon dating A dating method based on assessing the amount of radioactive carbon (C^{14}) remaining in a sample.

random sampling To choose a sample of a set of features (e.g. pits) using a statistical method which ensures that the features are chosen entirely at random.

spindle whorl Weight of stone or clay attached to a wooden spindle to provide momentum in the process of spinning.

terret ring Ring, usually of bronze, for joining horse harness.

Tertiary Geological time band representing the third of four blocks of time into which the geological past is divided.

trig-point A fixed point on a hill, established by the Ordnance Survey, for surveying the countryside.

Index

(Page numbers in **bold** indicate illustrations)

126

INDEX